⋆100⋆
AMAZING
AMERICANS

BY JEROME AGEL

Published by The Trumpet Club
a division of Bantam Doubleday Dell Publishing Group, Inc.
666 Fifth Avenue, New York, New York 10103

ISBN 0-440-84263-8

Printed in the United States of America
September 1990

10 9 8 7 6 5 4 3 2 1
OPM

⋆ 100 ⋆ AMAZING AMERICANS

HENRY AARON
ABIGAIL SMITH ADAMS
JOHN ADAMS
JANE ADDAMS
EDWIN ALDRIN, JR.
  (see Neil A.
  Armstrong)
SUSAN B. ANTHONY
NEIL A. ARMSTRONG
BENJAMIN BANNEKER
ALEXANDER GRAHAM
  BELL
SHIRLEY TEMPLE BLACK
RALPH BUNCHE
LUTHER BURBANK
AARON BURR
RICHARD EVELYN BYRD
RACHEL CARSON
ALEXANDER J.
  CARTWRIGHT
GEORGE WASHINGTON
  CARVER
WILT CHAMBERLAIN
WILLIAM CLARK
  (see Meriwether
  Lewis)

GROVER CLEVELAND
TY COBB
GEORGE ARMSTRONG
  CUSTER
JEFFERSON DAVIS
EUGENE VICTOR DEBS
JOHN DEERE
MILDRED ELLA
  DIDRIKSON
JOE DIMAGGIO
JIMMY DOOLITTLE
ABNER DOUBLEDAY
FREDERICK DOUGLASS
CHARLES RICHARD
  DREW
GERTRUDE EDERLE
THOMAS ALVA EDISON
GERALDINE FERRARO
GERALD R. FORD
HENRY FORD
ROBERT H. GODDARD
MARTHA GRAHAM
PETE GRAY
ALEXANDER HAMILTON
LORRAINE HANSBERRY
THOMAS JEFFERSON

WILLIAM LE BARON
  JENNEY
JOHN PAUL JONES
HELEN KELLER
JOSEPHINE GATES KELLY
FRANCIS SCOTT KEY
MARTIN LUTHER
  KING, JR.
JESSE WILLIAM LAZEAR
MERIWETHER LEWIS
ABRAHAM LINCOLN
CHARLES A. LINDBERGH
BELVA ANN LOCKWOOD
JOE LOUIS
DOUGLAS MACARTHUR
JAMES MADISON
WILMA MANKILLER
  (see Josephine Gates
  Kelly)
GEORGE PERKINS MARSH
GEORGE C. MARSHALL
JOHN MARSHALL
EDWIN MOSES
RICHARD M. NIXON
JOE NUXHALL
SANDRA DAY O'CONNOR
EUGENE O'NEILL
J. ROBERT OPPENHEIMER
JESSE OWENS
LINUS PAULING
JEANNETTE RANKIN
PAUL REVERE
SALLY K. RIDE

JACKIE ROBINSON
ELEANOR ROOSEVELT
FRANKLIN DELANO
  ROOSEVELT
BILL RUSSELL
DICK RUTAN
GEORGE HERMAN RUTH
JONAS SALK
DRED SCOTT
WILLIAM H. SEWARD
UPTON SINCLAIR
MARK SPITZ
HARRIET BEECHER
  STOWE
WILLIAM HOWARD TAFT
JIM THORPE
CLYDE TOMBAUGH
SOJOURNER TRUTH
HARRIET TUBMAN
GENE TUNNEY
JOHN TYLER
JOHNNY VANDER MEER
EARL WARREN
MERCY OTIS WARREN
GEORGE WASHINGTON
JAMES D. WATSON
NOAH WEBSTER
ELI WHITNEY
ORVILLE WRIGHT
WILBUR WRIGHT
  (see Orville Wright)
JEANA YEAGER
  (see Dick Rutan)

You will meet some old friends in this book and get to know some people for the first time. Almost every one of these 100 American men and women, boys and girls, familiar and new, have a common characteristic: They did something no one else had done—or has ever done—and they did it with courage, sparkle, innovation, integrity, and dedication.

They wore many hats: athlete, ecologist, tribal chief, soldiers, human-rights advocate, inventor, social crusader, President, dancer, and even plant breeder.

They made headlines: walking on the Moon . . . leading slaves to freedom . . . writing an entire dictionary . . . wiping out a deadly disease . . . discovering a planet . . . living alone in the deep freeze of Antarctica for 4½ months . . . hitting 755 major-league home runs . . . inventing the telephone. . . .

One of these amazing individuals was only a small child when she was one of the most popular people in the whole world. Another was 15 years old. Two were brothers. Another is still going strong in her mid-90s.

Their wonderful, fascinating stories are all here.

Henry "Hank" Aaron (born in 1934) hit more home runs than has any of the 13,000 other men who have played in baseball's major leagues. He is the King of Klout. In 23 seasons, he walloped 755 pitches out of the ballpark—at least 35 in each of 11 different years. He homered on the average of once every 16.38 official times at bat. When he hit his record-setting 715th career home run in 1974, passing Babe Ruth's total of 714, it was the greatest moment in baseball history.

Hammerin' Hank holds other records as well: most runs batted in, 2,297; most extra-base hits, 1,477; most total bases, 6,856. Pitching a fastball past him was said to have been like trying to get the morning sun up past a rooster's crow.

He was voted a league all-star 20 times with the Milwaukee/Atlanta Braves and once with the Milwaukee Brewers. He is the only athlete who has been honored on the floor of the United States House of Representatives. In the year he broke the home-run record, he was saluted by the Flag Day Committee of the House as "America's number-one athlete, a great competitor, and a sportsman in the finest American tradition . . . a humanitarian unsurpassed.'' He was also admired by Chief Justice of the United States Earl Warren, who said, ''Mr. Aaron plays with dignity and a quiet purposefulness. And *can* he hit that ball!''

Abigail Smith Adams (1744–1818) is considered by historians to have been the most important woman in the first decades of the United States. She ''was possessed of the history of our country and of the great occurrences in it.'' Over and over again, she called for the 13 American colonies to declare their independence from England.

In those days, women had few legal rights, and they were not represented in political meetings. Mrs. Adams urged her husband, John Adams (who became our second President, in 1797), and other Founding Fathers composing the Declaration of Independence to ''Remember the Ladies, and be more generous and favourable to them than your ancestors. . . . If perticuliar care and attention is not paid to the Ladies we are determined to foment a Rebelion. . . .''

Mrs. Adams called herself ''an eager gatherer'' of knowledge. She taught herself to read French and to become familiar with the literature of the English poets William Shakespeare, John Milton, and Alexander Pope. She attended lectures on science and was thrilled by the ''assemblage of Ideas entirely new. . . .''

President and Mrs. Adams were the first occupants of the unfinished President's House in the new capital city, Washington, D.C. The cavernous sandstone structure was made habitable only ''by fires in every part, thirteen of which we are obliged to keep daily, or sleep in wet and damp places." Mrs. Adams hung her laundry in "the great unfinished audience room."

Mrs. Adams believed that "youth is the proper season for observation and attention—a mind unincumbered with cares may seek instruction and draw improvement from all the objects which surround it. The earlier in life you accustome yourself to consider objects with attention, the easier will your progress be, and more sure and successfull your enterprizes."

John Adams (1735–1826), the first Vice President of the United States and our second President, made his reputation as a lawyer of integrity and courage when he defended British soldiers who had killed three Americans and wounded eight others in the Boston Massacre of 1770. He was opposed to England's harsh measures in the American colonies, but he made sure that the soldiers got a fair trial.

Mr. Adams gave birth to original and profound ideas on political affairs. He did not like being Vice President very much. He observed, "My country has in its wisdom contrived for me the most insignificant office that ever the invention of man contrived or his imagination conceived." As the number two man in the Washington Administration, he presided over the Senate; he cast 29 tie-breaking votes, still the record 2 centuries later.

He succeeded George Washington as President in 1797. He was the last Chief Executive to appear in person before Congress until our 28th, Woodrow Wilson, in the middle 1910s. President Adams was bitterly disappointed when he lost the election of 1800 to his

Vice President, Thomas Jefferson, and the two men did not speak to each other for a dozen years. Both President Adams and President Jefferson—two of our most influential Founding Fathers—coincidentally died on the very same day, which happened to be the 50th anniversary of the Declaration of Independence, July 4, 1826. The President at the time was John and Abigail Adams's son John Quincy Adams.

Jane Addams (1860–1935), the first American woman to be honored with the Nobel Peace Prize, was a leader of the Women's International League for Peace and Freedom and a distinguished social reformer. She was called a traitor by "superpatriots," the most dangerous woman in America, because she was antiwar. She didn't want the United States to join in the fighting and the destruction of the First World War in Europe.

Ms. Addams was a founder of one of the first social-reform, or welfare, settlements in the United States. In 1889 she converted a run-down mansion in an industrial area of Chicago into Hull-House, a community center for the poor. She wanted to help needy people improve their lives. She was convinced that they were "potentially useful citizens who simply needed help." Hull-House promoted neighborly cooperation. It exercised authority in the civic affairs of Chicago, and served as a model for the settlement movement all over the United States.

Ms. Addams, who was physically handicapped because of a crooked spine, was lovingly known to many as "St. Jane," a heroine, "a representative of the best that democracy can produce." She won the Nobel Prize in 1931. Her autobiographical book *Twenty Years at Hull-House,* published in 1910, is a landmark book dealing with social reform.

Susan B. Anthony (1820–1906) was born at a time when women could not vote or enroll in a university or own property or sign contracts or control their own income or even be the legal guardian of their own children. But she was convinced that men and women are equals, and she became one of the first advocates of women's rights.

Ms. Anthony gained national celebrity by voting—illegally—in the Presidential election of 1872, casting a ballot in Rochester, New York, for the reelection of President Ulysses S. Grant. She wanted to force the courts to decide if the new (1868) 14th Amendment to the Constitution defining citizenship gave women the right to vote. The Supreme Court, the highest court in the nation, ruled that the Amendment's equal-protection clause protected the citizenship of slaves freed after the Civil War of a few years earlier but did not give women the same privilege. Ms. Anthony was arrested for having voted, but she never paid the $100 fine, and she did not go to jail as ordered.

In the face of opposition and ridicule, the courageous suffragette (as a woman who promotes the right of women to vote is called) remained a vigorous leader for women's rights in politics, education, and industry: "Men, their rights and nothing more," she proclaimed; "women, their rights and nothing less."

In 1920, 14 years after Ms. Anthony had died, the states ratified the 19th Amendment, giving women constitutional protection for the right to vote. In 1984, a woman was the Vice Presidential candidate on the

Democratic national ticket. (See Geraldine Ferraro, page 30.)

Neil A. Armstrong (born in 1930) and **Edwin "Buzz" Aldrin, Jr.** (also born in 1930) are the first people ever to have set foot on the Moon. The American astronauts had rocketed away from Florida in *Apollo XI* at 7 miles per second, in order to escape Earth's gravity. Four days later, they crawled into the Moon-landing ship called the *Eagle* and sailed the remaining miles to Tranquility Base on the Moon.

Mr. Armstrong, who had flown 78 combat missions in the Korean war nearly 20 years earlier, put on his 183-pound life-support suit, which weighed only 30 pounds in Moon gravity. He backed out of the *Eagle*, gingerly descended a short ladder, and hopped onto the Moon. The world was glued to its television sets and saw Armstrong announce, "That's one small step for a man, one giant leap for mankind!" The historic date and time were Sunday, July 20, 1969, 10:56:20 P.M., eastern daylight time.

Astronauts Armstrong and Aldrin hopped around on the Moon like kangaroos. They found the surface to be fine and powdery. They planted the American flag and collected rocks. They erected a plaque that read, in part, "We came in peace for all mankind."

After 21 hours on the Moon, the astronauts reboarded the *Eagle* and blasted out to the *Apollo* command ship for the triumphant 238,000-mile return journey to Earth. President Richard M. Nixon called the epic odyssey "the greatest week in the history of the world since Creation."

Since the *Eagle*, 10 more astronauts—all American—have walked on the Moon.

Benjamin Banneker (1731–1806), a freeborn black man, helped to design the permanent capital of the United States. He was a member of the 6-man team that surveyed the 10-mile-square Federal Territory, now known as Washington, District of Columbia (D.C.).

Land in Maryland and Virginia had been assembled for $66 an acre. When the temperamental, prickly chief planner was fired by President George Washington and took his maps home with him, Mr. Banneker was able to reproduce from memory the exquisite drawings precisely. Government officials moved from the temporary capital in Philadelphia, Pennsylvania, to the city of "magnificent intentions" in 1801.

Mr. Banneker was a large man of noble appearance and uncommonly soft and gentlemanly manners. He did not have a formal education. He was a self-taught mathematical wizard. He was very inventive. He constructed what is thought to have been the first wooden clock made in America; it struck the hours unfailingly for 20 years. He was a naturalist, and the author of a series of almanacs for farmers and planters.

He sent an almanac to Vice President Thomas Jefferson, who wrote back to Mr. Banneker: "I thank you sincerely for your letter . . . and for the Almanac it contained. Nobody wishes more than I do to see such proofs as you exhibit, that nature has given to our black brethren, talents equal to those of the other colors of men, and that the appearance of a want of them is owing merely to the degraded condition of their existence, both in Africa and America. I can add with truth, that nobody wishes more ardently to see a good system commenced for raising the condition both of their body and mind to what it ought to be, as fast as the imbecility of their present existence, and other circumstances which cannot be neglected, will admit.''

Vice President Jefferson sent the Banneker almanac to the Academy of Sciences in Paris, which then honored the inventor with membership. The Vice President also arranged for Mr. Banneker's appointment to the capital survey team.

(If the District gains statehood, it would be renamed New Columbia.)

Alexander Graham Bell (1847–1922), whose lifelong work was teaching speech to the deaf, invented electrical transmission of speech—the telephone! It changed forever how people communicated with each other.

The first complete intelligible sentence was transmitted in Mr. Bell's residence in Boston, Massachusetts, in March, 1876. It passed through two closed doors via a wire between the transmitter in the laboratory and the receiver in the bedroom. The inventor, who was 29 years old, spoke into the transmitter: "Mr. Watson—come here—I want to see you," and his aide, Thomas A. Watson, came on the double. Later, the Scottish-born Mr. Bell sang "God Save the Queen" into the transmitter.

At the end of the year, Mr. Bell and Mr. Watson were carrying on conversations between Boston and Cambridge, 2 miles apart. Soon, Boston and New York City were talking with each other. By the end of the century, New York and Chicago were linked by telephone.

In January, 1915, Mr. Bell once again called, "Mr. Watson—come here—I want to see you," but this time Mr. Watson couldn't come right away. Mr. Bell was calling from New York and Mr. Watson was in California. It was the first transamerican telephone call. One hundred thirty thousand telephone poles carried 4 copper wires between 7 repeater, or booster, stations across 13 states from coast to coast.

Mr. Bell, a bearded, stout, bear of a man, was an eccentric and innovative genius. Among his designs was a rocket-powered airplane. His experimental model actually rose 30 feet and flew 75 feet. He tried to make an X-ray machine. When he was 72 years old, he set a speed record of 70 miles per hour in a hydrofoil boat. He never lost his childlike enthusiasm for, and fascination with, the world around him.

Shirley Temple Black (born in 1928) was once the most famous child in the world—with dimples, 56 golden curls, polka-dot dresses, and white tap shoes. She was given a special Oscar as the most popular movie personality of 1934, when she was 6 years old.

The 1930s were very hard times—they were economically depressed years—and Shirley Temple's films brightened the lives of millions: *Little Miss Marker, Poor Little Rich Girl, The Little Colonel, Heidi, Rebecca of Sunnybrook Farm*, and her very own favorite, *Wee Willie Winkie*. All are shown regularly on television and are available on videocassettes.

On her eighth birthday, Shirley received 167,000 presents.

She retired from the make-believe world of the movies when she was 22 years old. There had been two themes to her film career: the great love she had for her profession and the great love she had for her mother. "If I had to do it all over again, I wouldn't change anything," she has said. "I probably would have paid for the pleasure of working."

Mrs. Black is keenly interested in the real world. In 1969, she was a member of the United States delegation to the United Nations. She campaigned for lowering the voting age from 21 years to 18. (Teenage suffrage became law with the quick ratification by the states, in 1971, of the 26th Amendment to the Constitution.) From 1974 to 1976, she was United States Ambassador to the African nation of Ghana. She has said that Secretary of State Henry Kissinger was surprised "that I knew where Ghana was."

Mrs. Black was Chief of Protocol in the State Department, commanding a staff of 44. In 1989, she was appointed by President George Bush to be Ambassador to Czechoslovakia.

Ralph Bunche (1904–1971), who was born into poverty in Detroit and orphaned at the age of 13, was the first black to be awarded the Nobel Peace Prize. He was celebrated in 1950 for having negotiated the Four Armistice Agreements ending hostilities between Arab nations and the new state of Israel. Seventeen years later, he was named to the highest position ever held in the United Nations by an American—Undersecretary General for Special Political Affairs.

Dr. Bunche was also the first black to earn a doctor of philosophy degree (Ph.D.) in government from Harvard University (1934). He studied at the London School of Economics and at the University of Cape Town. He was a civil rights activist who risked his life many times to prove that no problem in human relations is insolvable.

Dr. Bunche was honored with a total of 37 honorary degrees. He lived by his grandmother's credo: Be honest with yourself and with the world.

Luther Burbank (1849–1926) had a green thumb. In his nursery in Massachusetts and later in California, the horticulturist (a person who raises and tends plants) bred 90 new varieties of vegetables and 113 new varieties of fruits and plants. He was sometimes criticized for "playing God," for "interfering with nature."

He made two blades of grass grow where only one had grown before. He transformed the color of the California poppy from golden to rose. It was said he had put "soul into a flower" when he gave fragrance to the calla lily.

Three achievements in particular made Mr. Burbank a benefactor to the human race. His new potato, an improvement on the ordinary tuber, was hailed as the greatest influence ever upon the food supply of the world, and it added tens of millions of dollars to the annual productive wealth of the United States. His spineless cactus became a valuable food for cattle in dry regions. And he created a pitless plum, which science had been convinced could not be done.

Mr. Burbank loved his work. "Can my thoughts be imagined," he wrote, "when, after so many years of patient care and labor, . . . I look upon these new forms of beauty on which other eyes have never gazed?"

Aaron Burr (1756–1836) was Vice President of the United States in 1804 when he shot dead the illustrious former Secretary of the Treasury Alexander Hamilton in an illegal duel of honor. The two men faced each other on a narrow ledge on the New Jersey shore of the Hudson River opposite New York City. Mr. Hamilton intentionally fired his shot wild. Mr. Burr deliberately shot at Mr. Hamilton, piercing his stomach.

For many years, Mr. Hamilton had been a burr under Mr. Burr's saddle. The two Revolutionary luminaries were sometime-friends but mostly political rivals disagreeing about most things. Mr. Hamilton was instrumental in making sure that Thomas Jefferson defeated Mr. Burr in the long-drawn-out Presidential election of 1800 (which had to be decided by the House of Representatives). He also made sure that Mr. Burr did not then become Governor of New York. Mr. Burr called for the duel so that he might avenge Mr. Hamilton's insults and injuries.

When Mr. Hamilton died in agony 28 hours after being shot, Mr. Burr fled seizure by legal authorities. In time, the charges and grand-jury indictments somehow faded away and were forgotten.

The assassin returned without fear of arrest to the new capital city of Washington, D.C. As Vice President, he was also president of the Senate in the Eighth Congress. He presided with impartiality, dignity, and skill over the trial of Supreme Court Justice Samuel Chase, who had been impeached by the House of Representatives. It was Mr. Burr's greatest service to the nation.

Richard Evelyn Byrd (1888–1957) was the first explorer to live and work alone in the vast, dark, snow-white region of Antarctica known as the Ross Ice Shelf. The Shelf, forced out over the large inlet called the Ross Sea, is hundreds of feet thick and equal in area to that of France.

Admiral Byrd lived for 4½ months in 1934 in a shack that had been built in a loft in Boston, Massachusetts, and shipped to Antarctica. The shack sat in an 8-foot-deep snow pit 15 feet long and 11 feet wide, out of the reach of hurricane-force winds and whirling snow-drifts. It was heated against minus-100-degree temperatures. The lone occupant was 400 miles away from a well-stocked camp and companionship. His mission was to observe and record the weather.

"I work in soundless torment," Admiral Byrd wrote in his diary. ". . . The silence of this place is as real and solid as sound." More real, in fact, than the occasional creaks of the ice and the heavier concussions of snow quakes.

He was nearly overcome by carbon monoxide fumes from his stove, which had become defective, and he had to be rescued.

Admiral Byrd was the most famous explorer of his time. He was fascinated by land beyond the horizon He went around the world when he was only 12 years old. After graduating from the United States Naval Academy, he crossed the Atlantic Ocean in a blimp. With three companions, he flew cargo nonstop from New York to Europe in the 3-motor airplane *America,* a few weeks after Charles Lindbergh had become the first person to fly alone across the Atlantic. With other companions on each flight, he was the first to fly over both the North Pole (1926) and the South Pole (1929).

Admiral Byrd's fearless pioneering explorations laid the groundwork for U.S. claims to potentially vast deposits of riches in the mysterious frozen world of

Antarctica, where scientists today are training for a mission to desolate Mars.

Rachel Carson (1907–1964), a gentle scholar and a reluctant crusader, changed the way the world looked at the world—that is, the way people viewed the environment. She alerted everyone to the dangers of the indiscriminate use of chemical pesticides and herbicides.

Ms. Carson's book *Silent Spring* (1964), first published in *The New Yorker* magazine, revealed that poisons used to kill harmful insects were also destroying the natural ecological balance of the planet. The population of countless species of birds had declined so fast since the introduction of DDT (the most widely used and most dangerous pesticide in those days) that Miss Carson foresaw the time when there would be no songs in the air.

"If we are going to live so intimately with these chemicals—eating and drinking them, taking them into the very marrow of our bones—we had better know something about their nature and power," Ms. Carson wrote.

She was a marine biologist and worked 16 years with the U.S. Bureau of Fisheries. She wrote three books about the sea, including the worldwide best seller *Sea Around Us* (1951). Her legacies include the establishment of the U.S. Environmental Protection Agency and the banning of DDT in agriculture.

Alexander J. Cartwright (1820–1892), a surveyor and an amateur athlete, designed the game of baseball as we know it today.

On the afternoon of June 19, 1846, in a park called Elysian Fields, in Hoboken, New Jersey, across the Hudson River from New York City, Mr. Cartwright supervised the layout of the perfect baseball diamond: 90 feet between each of the four bases—home plate to first base to second base to third base to home plate. He based the rules on the English game of rounders.

He was the umpire in the first game, which was between a squad of doctors, lawyers, and businessmen known as the Knickerbockers and a squad of clerks and blue-collar workers known as the New York Nine. There were about 100 spectators. The game ended after four innings, with the New York Nine winning by the score of 23 to 1. The second game of organized baseball wasn't recorded for another five years.

The seeds sown in Elysian Fields led to major-league baseball. The National League was created in 1876. The Western Association changed its name to the American League in 1900 and placed clubs in several eastern cities. In 1903, the first World Series was staged; the Boston American League team defeated the Pittsburgh National League team, five games to three.

George Washington Carver (c. 1864–1943) didn't learn to read and write until he was 20 years old. He was born a slave, and was once traded for a racehorse. Because he was black, he was not able to go to the schools he wanted to.

Against all odds, he became a world-famous agricultural chemist. Dr. Carver created 60 new products from the peanut. He said he merely tried to find out why the Creator had made the goober. Among the products made from the peanut were milk and coffee substitutes, bleach, wood stains, shaving cream, linoleum, and flour.

Dr. Carver made by-products of the sweet potato: molasses, flour, and vinegar. During the Second World War, he developed dyes of 500 different shades. When he took red clay and rich fertile soil known as loam and turned them into inks, pigments, cosmetics, papers, and paints, he said he was merely "releasing the potential already present in the environment."

Dr. Carver directed research at Tuskegee Institute, in Alabama, for a half century. He encouraged farmers to improve their soil by planting different crops from time to time. Reliance on cotton—King Cotton—was leaving the soil depleted and worthless; crop rotation, as Dr. Carver described the recommended practice, replenished the land, gave it new breath, new life.

Dr. Carver donated his life savings to the establishment of a foundation for continuing research in agriculture. His birthplace, at Diamond Grove, Missouri, is a national landmark.

Wilt Chamberlain (born in 1936) was a 7-foot-tall basketball player known as Wilt the Stilt and the Big Dipper. He once scored the incredible total of 100 points in a game. His teammates on the Philadelphia Warriors all together scored only 69 points during the Stilt's scoring rampage against the visiting New York Knickerbockers in a National Basketball Association clash in Hershey, Pennsylvania, in 1962. (Philly won by 22 points.)

Mr. Chamberlain scored 78 points in another game and at least 50 points in each of 118 other games during his 14-year professional career. Only a handful of players have scored over 60 points in a single game even once, and no one else has scored more than 73 points. He scored an average of 50.4 points a game in the 1961–1962 season.

In his very first NBA season, he set eight records and was named both Rookie of the Year and Most Valuable Player. In 1971–1972, he helped lead the Los Angeles Lakers to a record 33 consecutive victories.

The Big Dipper was the league scoring champion for seven consecutive years. He ended his career with 31,419 points—the record average of 30.1 points a game. He played almost every minute of 1,045 games—797 hours of running up and down the 90-foot-long court—yet he never once fouled out of a game, another remarkable accomplishment.

In addition to his scoring prowess, Mr. Chamberlain was a tiger on the backboards. He grabbed 23,924 rebounds. This means that he took possession of the ball for his team after nearly 24,000 missed shots.

Before joining the NBA, the Stilt had been an outstanding hoopster with the University of Kansas and with the Harlem Globetrotters.

Grover Cleveland (1837–1908) is the only President to serve two nonconsecutive terms. He was both our 22nd President and our 24th. He is also the only President to have been a hangman. He was a sheriff in Erie County, in northern New York, and personally put the noose around the neck of two murderers.

Mr. Cleveland was also a teacher of the blind, the Mayor of Buffalo, and the Governor of New York before becoming the first Democratic President (1885) since James Buchanan and the Civil War. Though President Cleveland won the popular vote in his reelection campaign, in 1888, he lost the Presidency because he lost the decisive states' electoral vote (233–168) to Republican Benjamin Harrison, grandson of our "one-month President," William Henry Harrison (March, 1841). Former President Cleveland ran again in 1892, and this time bested President Harrison (277–145).

Mr. Cleveland was the first President to veto more than 100 bills. In all, he vetoed 584 bills and became known as the "veto President." He is also the only President to be married in the White House. During his second Administration, he had a secret operation for cancer. Surgery on his upper jaw was performed on a yacht cruising New York City's East River. It was so secret an event that even President Cleveland's Vice President didn't know about it. The surgery was not made public until Mr. Cleveland died more than a decade later.

Ty Cobb (1886–1961) turned down the chance to attend the U.S. Military Academy in West Point, New York, choosing instead to play baseball. He became a superstar in the American League for 24 seasons. In 1936, he received the most votes in the first election of players to the National Baseball Hall of Fame—even more votes than the enormously popular Babe Ruth.

Mr. Cobb amassed numerous records in his 22 seasons with the Detroit Tigers and 2 with the Philadelphia Athletics. He was the league's batting-average champion 12 times. His career batting average of .367 is still tops in the major-league record book. His hit total of 4,191 is second only to Pete Rose's 4,256. In his last two campaigns, at the ages of 40 and 41, the left-hand hitting Mr. Cobb batted .357 and .323.

And he never slowed up. He stole a career total of 892 bases. "The Georgia Peach," in fact, was such a terror on the base paths, or so the story goes, that when he started to steal second base on the pitch to the batter, the catcher might throw the ball to third base to keep Mr. Cobb from stealing two bases at once!

George Armstrong Custer (1839–1876), who was graduated last in his class of 34 cadets at the U.S. Military Academy, became a Civil War hero-general in his early 20s. He demonstrated daring and brilliance in Union cavalry battles against the South at Bull Run and in the Peninsular Campaign. He was "gifted" with the oval-topped, varnished pine "surrender table" used by Generals Ulysses S. Grant and Robert E. Lee when the Confederacy surrendered at Appomattox Courthouse, Virginia, in early April, 1865.

After the war, the Army was reorganized, and General Custer was assigned to the rank of lieutenant colonel in the Seventh Cavalry. He took up duty on the frontier to help protect prospectors and settlers pushing farther and farther westward. In April, 1876, the Seventh Cavalry under Acting Commander Custer headed out from Fort Abraham Lincoln, in the Dakota Territory, and launched a surprise raid on several thousand Sioux warriors.

The attack backfired. The Indian war cry was "It is a good day to die," and Custer and his 266 men were wiped out on the slope of a hill at the Battle of the

Little Bighorn, in what is now southern Montana.

"Custer's Last Stand" was the Army's worst defeat in its wars with the Plains Indians. But President Theodore Roosevelt later said that General Custer's name was a shining light to all the youth of America: "His name reverberates like the clang of a sword."

Jefferson Davis (1808–1889) was a Mississippi Senator, popular in the North, when the 11 Southern slave states began seceding from the Union. He reluctantly helped to set up the Confederate States of America in revolt against President Abraham Lincoln and the Union.

Mr. Davis became the first president of the Confederacy, sitting first in Montgomery, Alabama, then in Richmond, Virginia. He was described by Mark Twain as "the head, the heart, and soul of the mightiest rebellion of modern times."

The Confederate constitution that president Davis helped to compose resembled the United States Constitution in many ways, but it recognized and protected slavery, the continuation of which was a major cause of the Civil War. Also, it called for a one-term presidency of 6 years.

During the last year of the Civil War, Mr. Davis was often in the field with his top general, Robert E. Lee. He was captured in Georgia a month after the South had surrendered at Appomattox Courthouse, Virginia, and held in irons in a federal military prison in Virginia. He was never brought to trial because of legal difficulties, and was finally released. He was given a hero's funeral in New Orleans.

Mr. Davis had been Secretary of War (1853–1857) in

President Franklin Pierce's Administration. Ironically, he built up the Union army and its capabilities—the very same army that later shattered his Confederacy.

Eugene Victor Debs (1855–1926), a labor organizer and a leader of the Socialist Party, received nearly a million votes in the Presidential election of 1920. (It was coincidentally the first time that women were allowed to vote.) What made the vote total phenomenal was the fact that Mr. Debs was behind bars in a federal prison in Atlanta, Georgia. He was in prison for having spoken out against the military draft and United States involvement in the First World War.

He ran for President 5 times. He netted 6 percent of all the votes in the 1912 election won by the Democrat Woodrow Wilson.

A socialist is a person who believes that "we the people" should own and operate the means of making and distributing things. Mr. Debs adopted socialism as a cause while he was jailed for having led worker strikes against railroads in the mid-1890s. He was an enormously popular man. "While there is a lower class, I am in it," he said: "while there is a criminal element, I am of it; while there is a soul in prison, I am not free."

Mr. Debs claimed that the federal government was "undermining the very foundation of political liberty and economic rights" and demanded a reorganization of the economic system according to socialist principles.

He was so popular that a public protest after the 1920 election prompted President Warren G. Harding to issue him a pardon and to invite him to the White House for a friendly chat and an official U.S. apology.

John Deere (1804–1886) invented a plow that made it possible to farm the vast fertile lands of Middle America profitably. It changed the course of agriculture for all time.

Mr. Deere had been a blacksmith in Vermont, where his highly polished hayforks and shovels were in great demand. When he moved to Illinois, he learned that the cast-iron plows carried west by the pioneers did not work well in the rich black soil of the prairies. The heavy soil clung to the wooden and iron moldboards designed for the sandy eastern soil; the earth had to be scraped off every few steps. (A moldboard is a curved plate, attached above a plowshare, which lifts and turns the soil.) Tilling, or preparing the land for seeding, was thus a slow, start-and-stop process.

In those days, the 1830s, nearly 90 percent of the estimated 15 million people in the United States were living on farms. But those in the West were beginning to quit the land in despair. There was not sufficient time during the growing season for farmers with cast-iron plows to harvest enough land to make a reasonable profit. At his smithy, or workshop, in Grand Detour, Illinois, Mr. Deere developed a steel plow that scoured itself clean and turned a clean furrow, or groove, in the soil. The time it took to plow a field was virtually halved.

Mr. Deere brought about the first large-scale manufacture and marketing of steel plows. Two decades later, his factory was turning out 10,000 plows a year.

Mildred Ella "Babe" Didrikson (1914–1956) wanted to be the greatest athlete in the world. She was by far the most outstanding woman athlete ever. She ran, threw, swam, jumped, boxed, bowled, fenced, skated, golfed, shot, and cycled. She played baseball, football, tennis, lacrosse, handball, and billiards. It was said that she was capable of winning everything except the Kentucky Derby. She was a one-woman team.

Physically, "Babe" was not a big woman. She stood 5 feet 4 inches tall and weighed only 105 pounds. She picked up her nickname because she could hit and throw a baseball like the great Babe Ruth. She also displayed another talent. As a teenager, she won first prize at a Texas state fair for a sports dress she had designed.

In the 1932 Olympic Games, in Los Angeles, California, she won gold medals in the javelin throw (a record of just over 143 feet) and the hurdles. She missed a third gold medal only because of a technicality; her method of high jumping had not been approved.

In 1943, she won 17 consecutive golf championships and became the first American to win the British Women's Amateur crown.

Joe DiMaggio (born in 1914), the star center fielder of the New York Yankees from 1936 to 1951, has been called the best team player in the history of major-league baseball. He holds the sport's most awesome record: He hit safely in 56 consecutive games.

During The Streak in the 1941 season, the "Yankee Clipper" banged out 91 hits, including 16 doubles, 4 triples, and 15 home runs. He scored 56 runs and drove in 55. He never once bunted to reach first base safely, and he struck out only seven times.

After going hitless in the 57th game, before a roaring

record nighttime crowd of 67,468 in Cleveland, Ohio, DiMaggio went on another consecutive-game hitting streak, this one for 16 games. He thus hit safely in 72 of 73 consecutive games. Awesome indeed!

"Joltin' Joe" was voted the Most Valuable Player in the American League three times.

Jimmy Doolittle (born in 1896) commanded 16 B-25 Army Air Force 2-engine bombers on a surprise raid on several major Japanese cities, including the capital city of Tokyo, in April, 1942. Four months earlier, Japan had sprung a devastating military strike at United States military bases in Pearl Harbor, Hawaii, while peace negotiations were going on in Washington, D.C. No one except American strategists thought that the United States could counterattack the Japanese mainland so soon after Pearl Harbor.

Each of Major Doolittle's planes took off with a 1-ton bomb from the deck of the new aircraft carrier *Hornet,* which was rocking around in heavy green seas 650 miles east of Japan. Their bombardment left a Japanese battleship in flames, smashed an airplane factory, and set fire to oil tanks. Most important of all, the mission raised the morale of all Americans. The war had been going badly for the United States. The Japanese army and navy seemed unstoppable. They were triumphant all over the Pacific and were expected to invade California.

The Doolittle raid was popularized in the movie *30 Seconds over Tokyo.* It is still one of this country's most celebrated military missions. Nearly 50 years after the event, Ronald W. Reagan referred to it in his farewell Presidential address to the nation: "We've got to teach history based not on what's in fashion but what's important," he said on nationwide television; we must all remember "who Jimmy Doolittle was, and what 30 seconds over Tokyo meant."

Abner Doubleday (1819–1893) is famous for something he didn't do. He did not invent baseball, but for nearly 100 years everyone believed that he had. He *did* organize ball games in Cooperstown, New York, in the late 1830s, and the talk that he had originated *base*ball eventually became what is today called "the Santa Claus story of baseball"—nice but not true. (Baseball was invented by Alexander J. Cartwright. See page 14.)

But Doubleday *did* do something that made him a celebrity, a hero in the Civil War. He fired back the first Union shot from Fort Sumter in the very first clash of the war, in April, 1861. Fort Sumter was a symbol of United States authority on an island in the harbor of Charleston, South Carolina, and Doubleday (a West Point graduate) was acting commander under Major Robert Anderson. The fort sent word to besieging Confederate troops that it would surrender when its food supply ran out in a couple of days. The Southern soldiers' sudden, unexpected response was to blast away at Sumter with cannon. Doubleday's initial return shot "bounced off from the sloping roof of the [ironclad] battery opposite without producing any apparent effect." No one was killed in the thundering exchange of cannonballs. (In fact, no Northern or Southern soldier was slain in the first 6 weeks of the war; then, 618,000 were, maybe more.) Doubleday and his men were captured, taken off the island, and allowed to sail north to New York City, where they were toasted with a heroes' welcome.

Doubleday went on to serve gallantly against Southern armies. He was one of the commanders in the Union victory at Gettysburg, Pennsylvania, which once and for all turned back the Confederates' invasion of the North.

Doubleday read French and Spanish literature and studied Sanskrit, the ancient sacred language of India. His nickname was "48 Hours," because he took so long to make a decision—he took a "double day."

Frederick Douglass (c. 1817–1895), who had suffered the humiliations and whippings of slavery, spent his life crusading for equal human rights and against racial injustice. He was the principal male participant in the first American women's rights convention, held in the bustling manufacturing community of Seneca Falls, New York, in 1848. During the Civil War, he met with President Abraham Lincoln and helped to recruit the glory-covered 54th and 55th Massachusetts black regiments for the Union.

As a child in Maryland, he wore a knee-length shirt, and on cold nights he slept in a corn bag. At the age of 21, he escaped to freedom in the North wearing the disguise of a sailor. His birth name had been Frederick Augustus Washington Bailey; as a free man, he gave himself the surname Douglass for a character in a novel by Sir Walter Scott.

He was an eloquent writer. His book about plantation life vividly suggests a life sentence in an uncommonly cruel prison camp. He campaigned in the North and in Great Britain for full freedom and full equality for all of his fellow blacks. "If there is no struggle," he said, "there is no progress."

Near the end of his heroic life, the 6-foot-tall advocate remembered his participation in the women's rights convention: "There are few facts in my humble history to which I look back with more satisfaction than to the fact, recorded in the history of the woman suffrage movement, that I was sufficiently enlightened at the early day, when only a few years from slavery, to support your resolution for woman suffrage. . . . When I ran away from slavery, it was for myself; when I advocated emancipation, it was for my people; but when I stood up for the rights of woman, self was out of the question, and I found a little nobility in the act."

His legacy is the awareness as to how injustice in its many forms oppresses all peoples of the United States—and the world.

Charles Richard Drew (1904–1950) was a pioneer in blood plasma research. He found an efficient way to store large quantities of blood plasma in "blood banks" for later use.

Dr. Drew supervised the American Red Cross blood-donor program during the Second World War, and he helped the British government establish the first blood bank in England. He was *the* authority on the subject of blood plasma.

In those times, the Red Cross segregated blood donated by non-Caucasians. Dr. Drew was black. His protests against discrimination and ignorance forced the Red Cross to change its rules. In 1944, Dr. Drew was awarded the Spingarn Medal of the National Association for the Advancement of Colored People (NAACP) for his contributions to science.

He became a professor of surgery at Howard University, in Washington, D.C., and helped black students with their medical training.

Dr. Drew had been an exemplary student in his undergraduate years at Amherst College, in Massachusetts. He won the Messman Trophy for bringing the most honor to Amherst during his four years there as both a scholar and an outstanding athlete (track and football).

Gertrude Ederle (born in 1906), who was already the winner of three medals in the 1924 Olympics and the setter of 29 national and amateur world records, was the first woman to swim the English Channel. "I just knew if it could be done, it had to be done, and I did it," she exulted.

Encased in three layers of grease, the chubby 19-year-old donned a red bathing dress, a skullcap, and goggles and plunged into the channel at Cape Gris-Nez, France, on the morning of August 6, 1926. Not since Spain's 130-ship "invincible" armada tried to invade England in 1588 had so many eyes been focused on that arm of the Atlantic Ocean, "the moat that nature herself built."

Ms. Ederle plowed through rain squalls and stinging sprays and running tides and heavy seas. Wireless messages of encouragement from her mother in New York were read to the swimmer by Ms. Ederle's father in a shepherding boat. He was his daughter's number one cheerleader: "Trudie, don't forget, you won't get that roadster unless you get there." She lifted her face out of the water and sputtered, "Pop, I will have that roadster." In the distance, huge bonfires on English beaches and the white cliffs of Dover beckoned.

With about 10 minutes to go before the tide would force her to quit, Ms. Ederle waded ashore, saying, "I did it for Mummy." Her time for the 21 miles was 14 hours and 31 minutes, which was 2 hours faster than any man had swum the channel since it was first conquered 51 years earlier. (Her record stood for 38 years.)

There was an unexpected postscript to the feat. At the docks in Dover, Ms. Ederle and her aides were grilled by an immigration official demanding passports and customs papers. He was booed by the deliriously happy gathering that had waited well into the night for a glimpse of their heroine.

Ms. Ederle returned to the United States (by ship) to a ticker-tape parade in New York City and an exuberant greeting by Mayor Jimmy Walker.

Thomas Alva Edison (1847–1931) transformed the everyday world as if by magic.

He was a scientific magician. He invented everything that came to mind in his New Jersey laboratories—and it seems almost everything did: the electric lamp and distribution system, the perfect phonograph, an electric vote recorder, a stock-report printer, an alkaline storage battery, a dictating machine, a mimeograph, the motion picture camera, and a fluoroscope for making X rays.

Mr. Edison considered the electric lamp his greatest achievement—it turned night into day. After completing an invention, he would jump up and down in excitement, in a kind of dance.

In all, he held 1,093 patents and composed 3.5 million pages of sketches, notes, and letters. His laboratory was a business for translating pure technology into commercial products. He wanted to learn and then use the "secrets of nature" for the "happiness of man." When his storage battery for electric automobiles didn't work, he recalled every one that he had sold and made a prompt refund from his own pocket.

Mr. Edison believed that genius was 1 percent inspiration and 99 percent perspiration. "Everything comes to him who hustles while he waits," he said. Curiosity dominated his habits. He had had only three months of formal education and he was nearly deaf; he couldn't hear a bird sing after he was 12 years old. Wide reading led him to his early technical and scientific pursuits.

"I always invent to obtain money to go on inventing," Mr. Edison used to say. When he died, many people the world over observed a voluntary "dim out" as a sign of respect.

Geraldine Ferraro (born in 1935) is the only woman ever nominated as a Vice Presidential candidate on a national ticket by a major political party in the United States. (No woman has been nominated for the Presidency by a major party.) She partnered the Democratic Presidential nominee, Walter Mondale, in the 1984 campaign. They didn't do very well. The ticket won the electoral votes of only Mr. Mondale's home state of Minnesota and the District of Columbia.

Ms. Ferraro was serving her third term as a U.S. Representative from Queens, New York, when she was tapped for the historic run by her party. She believes her candidacy was "a first step" for women in the national political spotlight: "It was a very tiny step, but people got used to seeing a woman talking about arms control, they got used to seeing a woman campaigning. . . . Emotionally, there was no more pressure on any candidate in the history of this country than there was on me. And I could handle it."

Gerald R. Ford (born in 1913) is the only person to be the Vice President and the President of the United States without being elected to either office.

President Richard M. Nixon—in the first use ever of the 25th Amendment to the Constitution—nominated, and Congress confirmed, Mr. Ford to replace Mr. Nixon's first Vice President, Spiro T. Agnew, who had resigned in a corruption scandal in October, 1973. When President Nixon himself resigned 10 months later as he was facing impeachment charges in the Watergate scandal (see page 53), Vice President Ford automatically became President.

Before becoming Vice President, Mr. Ford was a Michigan Congressman and the Republicans' minority leader in the House of Representatives. In 1976, he ran for a full term as President. He narrowly lost to the Democratic nominee, Jimmy Carter, a former Governor of Georgia.

Republican Senator Robert P. Griffin once said, "The nicest thing about Jerry Ford is that he just doesn't have enemies."

Henry Ford (1863–1947) put America on wheels. His Model T car, "the Tin Lizzie," was so low in price,

Mr. Ford said, "no man making a good salary will be unable to own one." The Ford company offered the Model T in any color, so long as it was black. More than 15 million Tin Lizzies were bought.

Mr. Ford, usually a meticulous planner, overlooked one important detail when he assembled his very first horseless carriage. The vehicle was larger than the door of the brick shed in which it had been built in secret! Workmen used the back of an axe to knock bricks out of the framework so the vehicle could make its entrance into the world. Within 17 years, one of every two cars in the world was a Ford. The company also made the first small tractor.

Mr. Ford was a combination inventor-industrialist. He created mass-production techniques and the conveyor-belt assembly line, which was a revolutionary innovation in manufacturing. He introduced a profit-sharing program for employees, who were already being paid more than the prevailing industry standard. The Ford Foundation became one of the major philanthropic institutions in the world.

Mr. Ford's lifelong motto was: The best fun follows a duty done.

Robert H. Goddard (1882–1945), a professor of physics and a pioneer in rocketry, predicted in 1926 that man would one day escape Earth's gravity and fly to the Moon. An editorial in *The New York Times* dismissed Goddard's claim that rockets could fly through space that didn't have any air.

In 1969, the *Times* apologized for its ignorance as American astronauts sailed 238,000 miles to the first landing on the Moon.

Dr. Goddard spent three decades experimenting with jet propulsion and sophisticated rockets. He published the first detailed correct theory of astronautics. He invented, built, and launched the first liquid-fuel rocket to fly under its own power. He was the first to suggest a staging concept—a two-step rocket. He became chief of the United States naval research on jet-propelled planes.

The Goddard Space Center, in Greenbelt, Maryland, is named in honor of the American "father of space travel."

Martha Graham (born in 1894), a direct descendant of the Pilgrim Miles Standish, invented a completely new art form—modern dance.

She maintains that dance was the first communication for all humans—the body does not lie, movement does not lie. "It's important that people feel," she says, "that they feel alive." She once looked at a slash of red paint against blue and said, "I will dance like that."

A supreme innovator, Ms. Graham is compared with the painter Pablo Picasso and the composer Igor Stravinsky because of the unquestionable dominance of her talent. She created 179 dances dramatizing life. Her masterpiece *Appalachian Spring* was made in 1944 to music composed by Aaron Copland.

"Artists are not ahead of their time," Ms. Graham has said, "they *are* their time." She believes that "we learn by practice, whether it means to learn to dance by practicing dancing or to live by practicing living." To her, there is only one sin: mediocrity.

Ms. Graham has been hailed as "a national treasure." She was the first dancer to be honored with the highest United States civilian honor, the Medal of Freedom. She retired from performance at the age of 75, in 1969, but she is still creative as she approaches her 100th birthday.

Pete Gray (born in 1917) lost his right arm in a wagon accident when he was 6 years old, but he overcame the handicap to play major-league baseball.

His original name was Peter Wyshner. He became the most valuable player in the Southern Association in 1944. The next year, he was called up to play center field for the St. Louis Browns (now the Baltimore Orioles) in the American League. The Second World War was still on, and there was a shortage of skilled players.

He played in 77 games in his one season with the Browns, 16 as a pinch hitter. He mustered a one-handed batting average of .218 in 247 plate appearances: 43 singles, 6 doubles, 2 triples. He struck out only 11 times and he walked 11 times.

He caught fly balls in his gloved left hand. He would then slip the glove into his right armpit, roll the ball across his chest to his left arm, and throw the ball back to the infield.

Pete Gray has not been the only handicapped player in the majors. Jim Abbott, who has only one hand, his left, now pitches for the California Angels in the American League. In his first season (1989), he won 12 games and lost 12 games.

Alexander Hamilton (1755–1804), a brilliant lawyer and George Washington's aide during the American

Revolution, recognized that the first charter of the United States—the Articles of Confederation, ratified by the states in 1781—wasn't working very well. He masterminded a meeting of delegates from 12 states that led to the drafting in 1787 of the Constitution of the United States, still "the supreme law of the land" more than 200 years later. He was not eligible to sign the Constitution, because a majority of delegates from his state of New York was not present, but he did so anyway.

Founding Father Hamilton was President Washington's first Secretary of the Treasury. He conceived programs to build the nation's financial reputation. In 1794, he and President Washington rode out at the head of 13,000 militiamen to force farmers in western Pennsylvania to pay federal taxes on home-distilled whiskey. Suppression of the Whiskey Rebellion demonstrated that the new national government had the authority to enforce its laws.

Mr. Hamilton was killed in an illegal duel with Vice President Aaron Burr (see page 12).

Lorraine Hansberry (1930–1965) was 28 years old when she became the first black woman to have a play produced on Broadway, *A Raisin in the Sun*. It was also her very first play. She was the youngest American and the first black playwright to win the Best Play Award from the New York Drama Critics' Circle.

Ms. Hansberry said that she was a writer who happened to be black and that *A Raisin in the Sun* is not a black play but a play about people who happen to be black. It is, she noted, the story of a family seeking a way out of a ghetto in Chicago, "the clash of the old and the new, but most of all [it is about] the unbelievable courage of the Negro people. It celebrates individuals who stand up for their own dignity and for others' dignity.''

Her plays *The Movement* (1964) and *The Sign in Sidney Brustein's Window* (1965) were also produced on Broadway.

Ms. Hansberry died of cancer at the age of 34.

Thomas Jefferson (1743–1826) wrote the inscription for his own tombstone: ''Here was buried Thomas Jefferson, author of the Declaration of Independence, of the Statute of Virginia for Religious Freedom, and Father of the University of Virginia.'' He chose not to mention that he had been two-term Governor of Virginia, Minister to France, Secretary of State under President George Washington, Vice President under President John Adams, and the two-term third President of the United States. Clearly, he thought of himself more as a philosopher, an idea man, than as a politician.

The Declaration of Independence (1776) reflects some of Jefferson's revolutionary ideas: Everybody is created equal . . . all of us are born with certain rights that can't be taken away . . . . these rights include life, liberty, and the pursuit of happiness . . . governments must get their just powers from the consent of the governed . . . whenever any form of government becomes destructive of these truths and rights, it is the right of the people to alter or abolish it, and to institute new government.

As President, Mr. Jefferson signed into law legislation prohibiting the importation of slaves after New

Year's Day, 1808. (The Continental Congress had eliminated from Mr. Jefferson's draft of the Declaration of Independence his criticism of England's support of the slave trade.) He authorized the Louisiana Purchase, doubling the size of the United States by 565,166,080 acres, paying Napoleon 2½ cents an acre.

Mr. Jefferson was a Renaissance man. His collection of 6,500 books became the core of the Library of Congress. He liked "the dreams of the future better than the history of the past."

William Le Baron Jenney (1832–1907), who had been a major in the engineers corps of the Union army in the Civil War, designed what most architectural commentators agree was the world's first skyscraper: the 16-story headquarters building for Chicago's Home Insurance Company in 1884–85.

The architect had traveled to Paris for training. He was inspired to design tall buildings when he observed how thin wires work as the frame for a bird cage.

Before Mr. Jenney's revolutionary design, massive walls held up buildings. The taller the building, the more massive the outer walls. Height, therefore, was restricted. Mr. Jenney wondered if a system of horizontal and vertical iron and steel beams inside the building could support the building and determine what it looked like. It could! The girders allowed buildings to soar into the sky, and they didn't need those fat outer walls.

The Home Insurance headquarters was the first structure of its kind to use steel as a building material, and it had the best plumbing system for a tall building up to that time.

Chicago was the birthplace of American architecture in the wake of the great Chicago Fire of 1871 which had destroyed most of the city. Many Chicago designers became world-famous: Louis Sullivan, Frank Lloyd Wright, Henry Hobson Richardson, and William Le Baron Jenney.

John Paul Jones (1747–1792) was the American commander in one of the fiercest and bloodiest naval battles in history. His outgunned, outmanned converted merchant ship *Bonhomme Richard* all but destroyed the British naval escort ship *Serapis* during the American War of Independence against Britain.

The two vessels were lashed together in a three-hour duel in moonlight off the coast of England in September, 1779. Their cannon fired at point-blank range. Captain Jones's answer to the *Serapis'* demand for surrender was "Sir, I have not yet begun to fight." When the *Serapis* raised the white flag, he transferred his men to the British ship and cut loose the *Bonhomme Richard,* which sank.

Captain Jones was the most famous and most successful officer in the Continental navy, the first to fly the American flag in combat at sea. He ranged over the Atlantic Ocean, from the Bahamas to the British Isles and France. He stole ashore in Scotland and disabled a fort's cannon and set fire to a coal ship. Congress awarded him the only gold medal granted to a Continental naval officer.

Captain Jones was born a British subject in Kirkcudbrightshire, Scotland. He fled to America after killing a mutinous crew member in self-defense. The adventurer's original name was simply John Paul. He took on the surname Jones in America. After the American Revolution, he went to Russia and served as a rear admiral in Empress Catherine's war with Turkey.

Helen Keller (1880–1968) is a symbol of the indomitable human spirit. She overcame the triple handicaps of deafness, blindness, and speechlessness caused by a childhood illness, probably scarlet fever. "Self-pity," she observed, "is our worst enemy, and if we yield to it, we can never do anything wise in the world."

At the age of 6, she sat on the knees of Alexander Graham Bell, the inventor of the telephone. (His wife was deaf, and he was a lifelong teacher of speech to the deaf. See page 8.) He understood Helen's rudimentary signs, and she knew it and loved him at once. "But I did not dream," Helen wrote years later in her autobiography, which was dedicated to Mr. Bell, "that that interview would be the door through which I would pass from darkness into light, from isolation to friendship, companionship, knowledge, love."

With the remarkable teacher Annie M. Sullivan (who was partially blind) at her side, Miss Keller was graduated from Radcliffe College, in Cambridge, Massachusetts, with honors in German and English. She traveled and "lectured" around the world. She would "speak" for a few minutes. Miss Sullivan, "the miracle worker," or "Teacher," as Miss Keller called her, would then repeat the remarks.

Miss Keller had "a happy life. My limitations never make me sad," she said. "I always felt I was using the five senses within me, that is why my life has been so full and complete. Perhaps there is just a touch of yearning at times. But it is vague, like a breeze among flowers. Then, as the wind passes, and the flowers are content . . . I can see a God-made world, not a man-made world.''

Josephine Gates Kelly (1888–1976) and **Wilma Mankiller** (born in 1945) are believed to be the first Native American women to be the leaders of their tribes.

Mrs. Kelly's tribe was the Standing Rock Sioux, whose reservation is in both North Dakota and South Dakota. She became its chief in 1943. She was a familiar sight in the legislative halls of Washington, D.C. She gained for Indians the right to hire legal counsel of their own choosing. It was a great triumph. (Formerly, the United States Bureau of Indian Affairs had appointed legal counsel for the tribes.)

Mrs. Kelly had seven children. She was a gold-star mother: Her youngest son, Louis, was killed in the Korean War and is buried in Arlington National Cemetery. Her granddaughter Susan Mary Power-Robinson became the first Native American woman to complete undergraduate work at Harvard University and to be graduated from Harvard Law School.

Wilma Mankiller was chosen chief of the Cherokee Nation, in Oklahoma, in 1985 after serving two years as deputy chief of the 67,000-member tribe. She says, ''It's like running a tiny, tiny country. I'm not real sure what we can learn from white society. The constant push for financial success, for position, for more money seems like a horrible waste of one's life. There is one thing, however, I do like about everyday American people: their willingness to help others.''

Francis Scott Key (1779–1843) was a lawyer in Maryland. He also wrote songs. One of the songs is our national anthem, "The Star-Spangled Banner."

During the War of 1812, Mr. Key stood on the deck of a British warship and watched it bombard the American Fort McHenry in Baltimore harbor. He was aboard the enemy warship under a flag of truce; he had been negotiating the release of a physician friend captured by the British when shelling erupted. He was so inspired by the fort's successful defense—by the dawn's early light he saw that its star-spangled banner was still there—that he wrote some descriptive eyewitness verses under the title "The Defence of Fort M'Henry." The patriotic song (the tune was popular British drinking music) quickly caught on throughout the new nation.

In 1815, Mr. Key retitled the song "The Star-Spangled Banner." The U. S. Navy adopted it as its anthem in 1889, and the Army adopted it in 1903. In 1931, "The Star-Spangled Banner" was adopted by Congress as the national anthem of the United States.

Martin Luther King, Jr. (1929–1968), a civil rights activist, a religious leader, and the president of the Southern Christian Leadership Conference, was honored with the Nobel Peace Prize in 1964. One of the most popular and important figures in the black protest movement in the United States, he led a series of nonviolent crusades: sit-ins, kneel-ins, wade-ins, freedom rides, and prayer meetings.

In August, 1963, more than 200,000 persons, white and black, marched in Washington, D.C., "for jobs and freedom." Dr. King's rousing, memorable "I have a dream'' speech on the steps of the Lincoln Memorial rang with hope for all Americans. ''One day this nation will rise up and live out the true meaning of its creed: 'We hold these truths to be self-evident: that all men are created equal.' . . . I have a dream that one day . . . little black boys and black girls will be able to join hands with little white boys and white girls and walk together as sisters and brothers. . . . I have a dream that one day even the state of Mississippi, a desert state sweltering with the heat of injustice and oppression, will be transformed into an oasis of freedom and justice. . . .''

Inspired by Dr. King, Congress renewed efforts to deal with the issues of civil rights and poverty.

In April, 1968, Dr. King traveled to Memphis, Tennessee, to help city workers, mostly black, improve the conditions of their jobs. He was murdered there by a white sniper, an escaped convict.

Dr. King's ''I have a dream'' speech echoes across the land to this day. It is read at gatherings on his birthday, January 15, now a national holiday.

Jesse William Lazear (1866–1900) surrendered his life to discover what caused the deadly disease yellow fever—and to make it possible to build the 50-mile-long Panama Canal, in Central America.

Dr. Lazear was a member of the United States Army Commission doing research into the cause of yellow fever in Cuba after the Spanish-American War of 1898. He allowed himself to be bitten by the kind of female mosquito thought to be the transmitter of the disease. He came down with fever, his skin turned yellowish, and he died.

Dr. Lazear's sacrifice helped to convince the commission that the mosquito, known technically as *Aedes aegypti*, was spreading the infectious disease. Eradication efforts could now be successfully directed.

Yellow fever had been a scourge in lands worldwide. It had struck major American cities. France's efforts in the 1880s to build a canal through Panama were turned back by yellow fever, which claimed 20,000 lives.

At the turn of the century, 1,400 cases of the disease were reported in Havana, Cuba. Within two years of Dr. Lazear's death, there wasn't a single case; yellow fever had been annihilated. When the United States took over construction of the canal linking the Atlantic and Pacific oceans, it was clear sailing!

Meriwether Lewis (1774–1809) and **William Clark** (1770–1838) were explorers who boldly went where no Americans had ever been before. *They* really discovered America.

Supported by a $2,500 grant authorized by Congress at President Thomas Jefferson's request, Lewis and Clark traveled across the recently purchased Louisiana Territory and into the unknown Northwest. Their commission was to find "the direct water communication from sea to sea and map rivers, study animals, plants, weather, minerals, and Indians."

Mr. Lewis was a diplomat and a scientific specialist. He had training in botany, zoology, and celestial navigation. Mr. Clark was a negotiator, an engineer, and a geographer. Intelligence was the principal reason for the success of the expedition.

The Lewis and Clark party of about 40 men in 3

well-stocked boats set out "under a jentle brease up the Missourie" River, in May, 1804. They crossed several ranges of the Rocky Mountains and sailed the Snake and the Columbia rivers and reached the Pacific Ocean in November, 1805. They established the U. S. claim in the Oregon territory.

Lewis and Clark completed their 4,000-mile round-trip in September, 1806, with the loss of only one man. There was national celebration. The explorers had discovered 24 Indian tribes (with whom they dealt with an unmatched record of decency), 178 plants, and 122 animals previously unknown to the civilized world. The stage was set for the new nation's westward expansion.

Abraham Lincoln (1809–1865) was one of the most revered American Presidents, and the first of four Presidents to be assassinated. He won the election of 1860 with only 40 percent of the popular vote.

Contrary to popular thought, his immediate goal was the preservation of the Union rather than the end of slavery. But on January 1, 1863, during the Civil War (1861–1865), he issued the Emancipation Proclamation. It abolished slavery in the rebellious Confederate states (but not where it was still practiced in the North). The President strongly supported a Constitutional amendment abolishing slavery everywhere in the country.

"Honest Abe" always believed that "the ballot is stronger than the bullet" and that "no man is good enough to govern another man without that other man's consent."

One month into his second term, only a few days after the Union had forced the Confederacy to surrender, President Lincoln was fatally shot in the back of the head as he watched a comedy in Ford's Theatre in Washington, D.C. The gunman was 26-year-old John Wilkes Booth, of the great theatrical family. He was a diehard Confederate sympathizer who earlier had plotted to kidnap Mr. Lincoln and carry him off to the Confederate capital of Richmond, Virginia.

"I want it said of me by those who knew me best," Mr. Lincoln once said, "that I always plucked a thistle and planted a flower where I thought a flower would grow."

Charles A. Lindbergh (1902–1974)—"The Lone Eagle"—was the first airman to fly all alone across the Atlantic Ocean. The year was 1927, only 24 years after the Wright brothers' first engine-driven flights in North Carolina.

A captain in the air corps reserve, Mr. Lindbergh took off in his single-engine Ryan monoplane *Spirit of St. Louis* (wing identification number N-X 211) from Roosevelt Field, on Long Island, New York. He landed 33½ hours and 3,600 miles later at Le Bourget, near Paris, France. He was a world hero, and the winner of a $25,000 prize for his historic flight. "Lucky Lindy" returned to the United States aboard a naval cruiser and was awarded the Medal of Honor. He was *Time* magazine's first Man of the Year.

Colonel Lindbergh had been a pilot in the experimental U.S. airmail service. He had to bail out three times in bad weather on the Chicago–St. Louis run. He warmed up for his transatlantic solo by piloting the

Spirit of St. Louis in record time (21 hours, 20 minutes) from San Diego, California, to Long Island, New York, making only one stop, in St. Louis, Missouri. During the Second World War, he flew on 50 combat missions in the Pacific theater.

In the early 1950s, his book about the unprecedented 1927 flight to Europe was honored with a Pulitzer Prize.

Near the end of his life, Mr. Lindbergh acknowledged that he liked birds more than he liked airplanes.

Belva Ann Lockwood (1830–1917) was the first woman to run seriously for the Presidency, and she ran twice. It was at a time when women did not have the right to vote in national elections. She was also the first woman to argue a case before the Supreme Court.

Mrs. Lockwood was the candidate of the National Equal Rights Party in 1884 and again in 1888. She asked, "Why not nominate women for important places? Is not [Queen] Victoria Empress of India? Have we not among our country women persons of as much ability and talent? Is not history full of precedents of women rulers?"

Mrs. Lockwood did not have an easy time getting her law degree. The National University Law School, in Washington, D.C., where she was living, would not admit her. She had to be tutored privately.

The Supreme Court, the highest court in the United States, at first did not allow her, or any woman, to argue a case before it. Mrs. Lockwood's persistence prompted Congress to pass a law enabling women lawyers to appear before the Court. She represented minority causes.

Mrs. Lockwood lobbied on behalf of legislation favorable to women. She was President Theodore Roosevelt's representative at international peace meetings in the early years of this century.

Joe Louis (1914–1981), the son of sharecroppers, was on his way to violin lessons when he was sidetracked to a gymnasium. The rest is boxing history.

From 1937 to 1949, the "Brown Bomber" was the world's heavyweight king. He defended his crown successfully 25 times.

Mr. Louis won the National Amateur Athletic Union light-heavyweight title in 1934 and immediately turned professional. Within three years, he was the heavyweight titleholder, winning the crown by knocking out the champion, James J. Braddock, in the eighth round. In a much-heralded bout in New York's Yankee Stadium in 1938, Mr. Louis in the very first round kayoed the only boxer to have defeated him, the German Max Schmeling.

Mr. Louis was a guest in the White House. President Franklin D. Roosevelt felt the fighter's biceps and remarked, "These are the types of muscles needed to beat Germany with." (At the time the Germany of Adolf Hitler was threatening world peace.)

Mr. Louis won 68 of his 71 professional bouts. He was a man of unfailing decency and dignity. By Executive Order, he was buried in Arlington National Cemetery with full military honors. It was always said that Joe Louis "was a credit to his race—the human race."

Douglas MacArthur (1880–1964) was the first general to win the Medal of Honor. He was hailed for his command of heroic American troops defending the Philippines in the Far East during Japan's invasion in the early months of the Second World War. (Nearly a century earlier, his father had won the Medal of Honor for gallantry during the Civil War.)

He was the top man in his class at the U.S. Military Academy at West Point, New York (1903), and he was superintendent there for three years (1919–1922). He was America's best frontline general in Europe in the First World War.

When the Philippines surrendered in the spring of 1942, Lieutenant General MacArthur escaped by PT boat to Australia, vowing, "I shall return." He did, wading ashore at Leyte 2½ years later. (The Battle of Leyte Gulf in October, 1944, was the largest naval action ever waged; the Allies devastated the Japanese navy.)

General MacArthur was a five-star general when he accepted Japan's unconditional surrender aboard the United States battleship *Missouri* anchored in Tokyo Bay, on September 2, 1945.

He was the first commander of United Nations troops fighting Communist North Korean and Chinese armies in the Korean War in 1950. He was relieved of his duties in 1951 by *his* commander in chief, President Harry S. Truman, for public criticism of the President's conduct of the war.

"Big Mac" returned to the United States a national hero. He was celebrated in a spectacular ticker-tape parade in New York City in April, 1951; an estimated 3,249 tons of paper rained down on the motorcade. He told a cheering joint session of Congress, "Old soldiers never die, they just fade away."

James Madison (1751–1836) has been called "the father of the Constitution," and he was the principal architect of the first 10 amendments to the Constitution—the Bill of Rights.

He went to the Constitutional Convention in Philadelphia, Pennsylvania, in the summer of 1787 believing that the new United States would have a more stable, more durable national government if it rested on the solid foundation of "we the people." After the Constitution was composed, he wrote nearly 30 newspaper essays supporting its ratification, or approval, by the states. He reminded his readers, "what is government itself but the greatest of all reflections on human nature? If men were angels, no government would be necessary."

Mr. Madison represented the state of Virginia in the first four Houses of Representatives (1789–1797). He served as President Thomas Jefferson's Secretary of State and succeeded Mr. Jefferson as President (1809–1817).

During his second Presidential term, President Madison fled Washington, D.C., when British troops set fire to both the Capitol and the White House in the War of 1812, America's "second war of independence."

During the Constitutional Convention, Mr. Madison used a self-taught system of shorthand to make the most extensive notes of any of the 55 delegates from 12 states. He requested that his recordings not be published until the last delegate had died. That last delegate turned out to be Mr. Madison himself. His widow, Dolley Madison, sold the papers to the government for about $30,000 and a lifetime pension.

George Perkins Marsh (1801–1882) had both the perfect surname—Marsh—for being the world's first celebrated ecologist, and the perfect hometown name: Woodstock, in the Green Mountains of Vermont.

He correctly predicted that the invention of the silk hat would cause the formation of many small lakes and bogs in the United States. The reason: There would be a reduced demand for beaver furs, and beavers in large enough quantities would again set about their business of reshaping geography.

Mr. Marsh always saw the trees for the forest. His book *Man and Nature: Or, Physical Geography as Modified by Human Action* was published in 1864 and is a classic. He described the fragility of nature, and argued that nature must be respected:

"Man has too long forgotten that the earth was not given to him for consumption, still less for profligate waste . . . the multiplying population, the impoverished resources of the globe, demand new triumphs of mind over matter." His insights led to the enactment of conservation policies in the United States.

Mr. Marsh was a diplomat and a linguist, and very much a concerned citizen. He contributed entries to the first *Oxford English Dictionary*. The 20 languages he spoke came in handy when he represented the United States in foreign ministries.

George C. Marshall (1880–1959) has been saluted as one of the greatest military geniuses in the history of the United States Army. He was a staff officer with the American Expeditionary Force in Europe during the First World War and Chief of Staff of the entire 7-million-man army during the Second World War.

General Marshall gained universal praise for a program he put forward as President Harry S. Truman's

Secretary of State after the Second World War. In a commencement address at Harvard University in 1947, he proposed the $13.3 billion "Marshall Plan" to help devastated European countries "willing to assist in the task of recovery" to get back on their feet, to escape hunger, poverty, despotism, and chaos:

"We must not fail to meet this inspiring challenge. We must not permit the free community of Europe to be extinguished. Should this occur, it would be a tragedy for the world. It would impose incalculable burdens upon this country and force serious readjustments in our traditional way of life. One of our important freedoms—freedom of choice in both domestic and foreign affairs—would be dramatically curtailed. Whether we like it or not, we find ourselves, our Nation, in a world position of vast responsibility. We can act for our own good by acting for the world's good."

General Marshall later served as president of the American Red Cross.

If he hadn't been a military leader, General Marshall would have liked to have been the conductor of a symphony orchestra.

John Marshall (1755–1835) was Chief Justice of the United States for 34 years, a tenure that spanned six Presidencies. It is the longest time that any of the 16 Chief Justices has held the highest position in the legal profession. Mr. Chief Justice Marshall's opinions and determination made the Supreme Court into a vital third branch of a strong, effective central government. They helped to bring together an expanding nation of totally different states.

Mr. Chief Justice Marshall claimed successfully that the Supreme Court—and all federal courts—had the power of judicial review. The Supreme Court could declare unconstitutional and unenforceable a federal or state law or other governmental action not in agreement with it. He wrote,

". . . The particular phraseology of the Constitution of the United States confirms and strengthens the principle, supposed to be essential to all written constitutions, that a law repugnant to the constitution is void; and that courts, as well as other departments, are bound by that instrument."

The Court would have the last word, unless the people of the United States, acting through Congress and the state legislatures, chose to override the Court by adopting a Constitutional amendment.

Legend has it that the Liberty Bell cracked tolling the death of Mr. Chief Justice Marshall, considered to this day the greatest of all our Chief Justices.

Edwin Moses (born in 1953) holds the longest winning streak in the history of track.

A graduate of Morehouse College, in Atlanta, Georgia, he won 122 consecutive races in the high hurdles. The streak ended on June 4, 1987, when he was nipped by one-thirteenth of a second by another American, Danny Harris, in the 400-meter hurdles at an international meet in Madrid, Spain. He had not lost a high-hurdles race for 10 years.

The 400-meter hurdles event has 10 hurdles. Winning requires strength and precision as well as speed. In 1976, Mr. Moses set the Olympic record in the event with a time of 47.64 seconds. He won another gold medal in the 1984 Olympics. (The United States did not compete in the 1980 Olympics in Moscow.)

Mr. Moses chalked up 12 of the first 15 times below 47.50 recorded for the 400.

He was the first United States athlete to be chosen as a delegate to the International Amateur Athletic Union.

Richard M. Nixon (born in 1913) is the only President of the United States to resign.

He quit in August, 1974, in the middle of his second 4-year term. He was facing three articles of impeachment by Congress; he was accused of not telling the truth about his knowledge of the break-in at the Democratic Party's national headquarters in the Watergate complex in Washington, D.C., during his successful reelection campaign in 1972.

(The burglars were connected with Mr. Nixon's Republican campaign staff. The President was deeply involved in the cover-up conspiracy, but this was not learned publicly until he had won the election by a landslide over the Democratic candidate, Senator George McGovern. The Supreme Court ruled that the President must uphold the law and is himself not above the law.)

Mr. Nixon received from his successor, President Gerald R. Ford, a full, complete, and absolute pardon for any crimes he had committed or may have committed. Mr. Ford's gesture is controversial to this day.

Mr. Nixon had been President Dwight D. Eisenhower's Vice President, from 1953 to 1961. He lost the Presidential race to John F. Kennedy in 1960 and the race for the governorship of California two years later. He still had the political itch. He bounced back onto

the national scene in 1968, defeating Vice President
Hubert H. Humphrey for the Presidency.

Mr. Nixon's Presidency will also be remembered
for a spectacular diplomatic overture. A lifelong foe of
communism, he was able to recognize the importance
of bringing the Communistic People's Republic of
China into the world community. His memorable
"journey for peace" to China improved relations between the Asian giant and the free world. Similar
uncharacteristic events are now referred to as "the
Nixon-in-China syndrome."

Joe Nuxhall (born in 1928) was the youngest player
ever to be in a major-league baseball game.

He was 15 years old and a student in high school in
Hamilton, Ohio, when he walked out of the Cincinnati
Reds bullpen on the afternoon of June 10, 1944, to
pitch against the St. Louis Cardinals. Four days earlier, Allied armies had finally crossed the English
Channel and invaded Hitler's Western Europe. The
Second World War had depleted the rosters of the
baseball clubs; talent was in short supply. Young Joe,
with high-school pitching experience, was drafted by
the Reds to help fill the gap.

The Cardinals were leading, 13–0, in the ninth inning, when Reds' manager Bill McKechnie told "the
kid" to go out there and pitch.

"The kid" lasted only two-thirds of an inning. He
walked five Cardinals, he threw one wild pitch, and he
gave up two singles and five runs. As he walked off
the mound for still another relief pitcher, he stumbled
and fell flat on his face. (The Cardinals' 18–0 triumph
was the most one-sided shutout in the National League

for 38 years, but they tied a negative record by leaving 18 men on base.)

Mr. Nuxhall didn't play in the majors again for 8 years, then pitched for 15 seasons, winning 135 games. He became a sportscaster for the Reds.

Sandra Day O'Connor (born in 1930), whose childhood ambition was to be a cattle rancher, is the first woman to sit on the Supreme Court of the United States. (There have been 103 male justices.) She was nominated in 1981 by President Ronald W. Reagan, who was fulfilling a campaign promise to name a woman to the highest court in the land. She received the confirming approval of all but 9 of the 100 Senators.

Justice O'Connor had served in all three branches of the Arizona government: assistant Attorney General, Senate majority leader (the first woman elected to that post in any state), and trial judge and appellate judge.

She was graduated third in her law class of 102 students at Stanford University in 1952. (Ranking first in the class was William H. Rehnquist, the current Chief Justice.) She believes the Founding Fathers might be "pretty surprised that the law of the land was being interpreted by a woman." (Women were not represented at the Federal Convention, which framed the Constitution more than 200 years ago.)

Justice O'Connor sees the role of the Court as trying to develop a reasonably uniform and consistent body of federal law: "I still tend to believe that the best government is that government closest to the people." In 1988, she reacted to a suggestion that she be the

Republican Vice Presidential candidate by declaring, "I most assuredly am not considering any other position in or out of government and do not expect to do so in the future."

Eugene O'Neill (1888–1953), the son of an actor, has been the nation's most honored playwright. He won four Pulitzer Prizes and a Nobel Prize. His genius lay in the boldness of his dramas.

The drama critic of *The New York Times* observed that "O'Neill's face is marked with experience. It is not tired. It is vivid; there is something immediately magnetic about his personality. He has the physical strength of one who understands the strength of nature . . . he is gentle and sympathetic. . . ."

Mr. O'Neill won Pulitzers for the dramas *Strange Interlude* (1928), which takes five hours to perform; *Beyond the Horizon* (1920); *Anna Christie* (1922); and *Long Day's Journey into Night*, which was written in 1941 but not performed until 1956. In 1936, he became the first American playwright to be awarded a Nobel Prize for literature.

Many critics believe his masterpiece is the 13-act trilogy *Mourning Becomes Electra* (1931). Set in post–Civil War New England, it is a retelling of an ancient Greek story of the murder of a husband by his wife and the revenge and guilt of their children.

As he neared the end of his life, Mr. O'Neill burned uncompleted manuscripts of a nine-play cycle he called *A Tale of Possessors Self-Dispossessed*. He had worked on the plays from the mid-1930s. A draft of the sixth play in the series, *More Stately Mansions,* was salvaged, and it was produced in Los Angeles, California, in 1967.

The playwright lived in a house built 2,800 feet up into the side of a mountain 35 miles north of San Francisco, California. He called it Tao House, meaning "the right way of life" in Chinese. It is today a national historic site, preserved solely because of its place in literary history.

J. Robert Oppenheimer (1904–1967) has been called "the father of the atomic bomb." He was the physicist who coordinated its development in two tension-filled years during the Second World War. Two of the three Axis powers, Germany and Italy, had already surrendered when the first atomic bomb, called simply "the gadget," was tested in the desert at Trinity Site, near Alamogordo, New Mexico, on July 16, 1945. Scientists believed there was 1 chance in 30 that the superbomb would obliterate the entire state.

Dr. Oppenheimer argued that the 6-year war would be brought to a hasty conclusion if A-bombs were dropped without warning on Japan, the last of the Axis powers still in the war they had started. In early August, 1945, the last two such bombs in the United States arsenal were dropped from B-29 Superfortress planes. They wiped out the cities of Hiroshima and Nagasaki, killing 105,000 Japanese in a flash. Emperor Hirohito surrendered.

Dr. Oppenheimer, on both technical and moral grounds, vigorously opposed the development of the far more lethal hydrogen bomb. He lost that argument. (The H-bomb, which is triggered by the explosion of an A-bomb, is today the world's mightiest explosive.)

Dr. Oppenheimer wrote the Baruch Plan for control

of atomic energy by the United States. He was honored with the Atomic Energy Commission's Fermi Award for "his outstanding contributions to theoretical physics and his scientific and administrative leadership."

He always maintained that "there are children playing in the street who could solve some of my top problems in physics, because they have modes of sensory perception that I lost long ago."

Jesse Owens (1913–1980), the track and field star of the century, tied one record and set three world records within 45 minutes at the Big Ten Championships in Ann Arbor, Michigan, on May 25, 1935. He was a student at Ohio State University and was called "the Ebony Antelope."

In 1936, his last year in competition, "the fastest man alive" streaked to four gold medals and set three records in the Olympic Games in Berlin, Germany. He won the 100- and the 200-meter sprints and the running broad jump (26 feet, 5 inches), and he was the anchor on the United States 400-meter relay team. (The United States finished second to Nazi Germany in team totals in the Games.)

In West Berlin today, there is a Jesse Owens Avenue. It leads straight to the city's Olympic Stadium.

"There is no difference between the races," Mr. Owens insisted. "If the black athlete has been better than his white counterpart, it's because he is hungrier—he wants it more."

In 1990, the great sprinter and long jumper was honored with a gold medal for "humanitarian contributions in the race of life." It was presented to his widow by President George Bush, who described Mr. Owens as an "Olympic hero and an American hero every day of his life, born with the gift of burning speed. He was always the fastest."

Linus Pauling (born in 1901), the son of a druggist, is the only person to win two Nobel Prizes all by himself. Most Nobels are shared by partners in accomplishment.

In 1954, Dr. Pauling won the esteemed prize for chemistry, for his work on chemical bonds and molecular structure.

He won the Nobel Peace Prize in 1962 for his warnings about the dangers of nuclear fallout and for urging an end to the testing of nuclear weapons.

Dr. Pauling revolutionized thinking concerning the structure of molecules. He was close to being the first scientist to unravel the DNA code—the genetic building blocks of life. His 1939 book, *The Nature of the Chemical Bond,* has been one of the most influential chemical texts of the century.

Dr. Pauling believes that large dosages of vitamin C can ward off and even conquer the common cold and other illnesses. He takes 3,000 milligrams every day.

"Science is the search for truth," Dr. Pauling said in *No More War!* in 1958, "it is not a game in which one tries to beat his opponent, to do harm to others. We need to have the spirit of science in international affairs, to make the conduct of international affairs the effort to find the right solution, the just solution of international problems, not the effort by each nation to get the better of other nations, to do harm to them when it is possible."

Jeannette Rankin (1880–1973), who was born near Missoula, Montana, was a lifelong ardent feminist and pacifist. She lived to be 92 years old.

Ms. Rankin was the first woman member of the U.S. House of Representatives, and the only member of either the House or the U.S. Senate to vote against the entry of the United States into both the First World War (1917) and the Second World War (1941).

She had been elected as a Republican member of the House in 1916 after leading a successful campaign for a woman's right to vote in Montana. She lost her seat in 1918. For the next 22 years, she was a social worker, and she lectured widely. In 1940, she was reelected to the House as an Independent for one term.

In 1968, when Ms. Rankin was nearly 90 years old, she was still fighting for peace. She led the Jeannette Rankin Brigade of 5,000 women in a march on Capitol Hill, in Washington, D.C., to protest United States involvement in the civil war in Vietnam.

Paul Revere (1734–1818) was the first of 12 children and was himself a dedicated family man, the father of 16 children. He was a master silversmith, an engraver, a dentist, and the owner of a silver shop, a hardware store, and a bell and cannon foundry. He is best known as a Boston patriot, the Son of Liberty immortalized in Henry Wadsworth Longfellow's poem *Paul Revere's Ride* (1861), warning the Middlesex (Massachusetts) countryside that the British were coming!

Literally on the eve of the American Revolution, Mr. Revere "called upon a friend, and desired him to make the Signals. I then went Home, took my Boots and Surtour, and went to the North part of the Town, where I had kept a Boat; two friends rowed me across the Charles River. . . . I set off upon a very good Horse . . .'' borrowed from a deacon. He alerted each household along the road that British soldiers were on the march. He reached Lexington and warned the superpatriots John Hancock and Samuel Adams. He planned to go on to Concord, but was stopped by a Redcoat patrol, which took away his horse. The following morning—April 19, 1775—the 13 American colonies' war for independence from England exploded. Militiamen from the countryside, in the battles of Lexington and Concord, fired shots heard 'round the world.

Mr. Revere fought the French at Lake George, New York, in 1756, in the French and Indian War. He was a courier for Boston's Committee of Correspondence, speeding dispatches as far south as Philadelphia, Pennsylvania. His political engravings stirred up patriotic sentiments. His most famous one is of the Boston Massacre (1770), the shooting of 11 citizens by British soldiers.

He was one of the colonists who put on crude disguises, boarded three British ships, and threw 340 casks of low-priced tea into Boston Harbor—the Boston Tea Party, of December, 1773.

Sally K. Ride (born in 1951), when she was a teenager, thought about becoming a professional tennis player. She became a physics researcher instead—and America's first woman astronaut.

In 1983, Ms. Ride was a mission specialist on the 6-day, seventh flight of the space shuttle in Earth orbit.

She operated the 50-foot robotic arm that retrieved a 3,000-pound satellite from space. "The thing I'll remember most about the flight is that it was fun," she said in the debriefing. Fifty-seven men in the NASA program had preceded her into space, as had two Soviet women, one of them nearly 20 years earlier.

Ms. Ride went into space again the next year. She deployed an Earth-observation satellite in an 8-day mission. She jogged on a treadmill for exercise. She joked that she was probably the only person ever to run across the Indian Ocean.

She left the space program in 1987 to join the Stanford University Center for International Security and Arms Control, in Palo Alto, California. She moved to San Diego and became the director of the California Space Institute of Oceanography and a professor of physics at the University of California.

Jackie Robinson (1919–1972) was major-league baseball's first black player. He is admired today for his courage and virtue. He was one of the best all-around athletes of the 13,000 who have played in the big leagues. His picture is on a postage stamp and he is a popular subject with schoolchildren writing papers for class.

In high school and college in California, he was a baseball, football, basketball, and track star. During the Second World War, he was a lieutenant in the army. He defied segregation rules at his Texas base by refusing to move to the back of the bus, where blacks were forced to sit. He was court-martialed but not convicted. "I was in two wars," he later said, "one against a foreign enemy, the other against prejudice at home.''

Mr. Robinson broke the color, or white-only, barrier in baseball when he was offered a contract with the Montreal Royals farm team of the Brooklyn Dodgers.

He played one season (1946) with Montreal in the International League, and was voted the circuit's most valuable player. In 1947, he was promoted to play second base for the Dodgers in the National League. Some teams threatened to strike, and many of Robinson's teammates wanted nothing to do with him. But he was so good a player that he won the Rookie of the Year honor with 175 hits and a .297 batting average, and he had the fortitude to ignore racial slurs and insults. In 1949, he batted .342 and became the first black to win the National League's Most Valuable Player award. He helped to lead the Dodgers to 6 pennants in the 10 years he played. He was the unconquerable doing the impossible, a hero for mankind.

Five years after hanging up his spikes, Jackie Robinson became the first black in the National Baseball Hall of Fame. Today, at least 25 percent of major-league baseballers are black.

Eleanor Roosevelt (1884–1962) was voted ''our most distinguished First Lady'' by 100 American history professors. They agreed that no other First Lady, or President's wife, ''has had her influence, no other has been so much the center of controversy, and no other has so affected the lives of the women who followed her.'' President Harry S Truman called her ''the first lady of the world.'' Her picture appears on postage stamps of many countries.

Mrs. Roosevelt was the wife of our only four-time President, her distant cousin Franklin Delano Roosevelt. When he became crippled by polio, she began traveling the country as her husband's "eyes and ears." In a lecture in Akron, Ohio, she was asked, "Do you think your husband's illness has affected his mentality?" She replied clearly and slowly, "I am glad that question was asked. The answer is yes. Anyone who has gone through great suffering is bound to have a greater sympathy and understanding of the problems of mankind." She received a standing ovation.

She corresponded with people of all ages everywhere in the world. One of her pen pals was convinced that America's greatest President was "Franklin Eleanor Roosevelt," which was a play on her husband's middle name, "Delano."

Mrs. Roosevelt twice represented the United States in the United Nations, working hard as always on behalf of war refugees. She was chairman of the U.S. Commission on Human Rights for 5 years. She believed that "no one can make you feel inferior without your consent."

Franklin Delano Roosevelt (1882–1945) is the only President to have served more than two terms. He was elected to unprecedented third and fourth terms in 1940 and 1944. Less than three months after being sworn for the fourth time, in the only inauguration ever held in the White House, our 32nd Chief Executive died of a brain hemorrhage while on vacation in Georgia. He had been President for 145 months, including 40 of United States action in the Second World War.

FDR, as he was referred to by newspaper headline writers short of space, became paralyzed from the waist down at the age of 39. He had caught the dread disease polio. The year was 1921. He was never able to walk again without braces or other aids. He once said, "If you've spent two years in bed trying to wiggle your toes, then anything else seems easy."

In spite of his handicap, Mr. Roosevelt bounced back into the political ring. (He had been the Democratic Party's nominee for Vice President in 1920.) He became Governor of New York, and in 1932 he became the first Presidential candidate to accept the nomination in person at his party's convention rather than follow tradition and acknowledge the honor by mail weeks later. He wanted to show both his fellow Democrats meeting in Chicago and the nation's voters that he was "up" to the Presidency.

His theme was "a New Deal for the American people." He preached four freedoms for all Americans: of speech and of worship, from want and from fear.

Bill Russell (born in 1934) is the first black to have coached a modern major-league sports team. He had been an outstanding basketball player in college and in the National Basketball Association.

A 6-foot 10-inch center, he had sparked the University of San Francisco Dons to 55 straight victories and national collegiate basketball championships in 1955 and 1956. He then led the American Olympic basketball team to a gold medal in Melbourne, Australia, in 1956.

The ball also bounced well in Mr. Russell's court in

the NBA. He was the league's most productive player as the Boston Celtics won eight straight championships. He was a ferocious defender. He grabbed 51 rebounds in one game. He blocked shots. He triggered the Celts' fast-break offense.

"Russ" was promoted to player-coach of the Celtics in 1966 and the team won two more championships. He was voted the NBA's Most Valuable Player five times. He went on to coach the Seattle SuperSonics for 4 years in the 1970s and to become vice president of the Sacramento Kings.

He has refused induction into the Basketball Hall of Fame, probably because he believed black players had suffered discrimination at the hands of white coaches, owners, and the public.

Dick Rutan (born in 1938) and **Jeana Yeager** (born in 1952) plucked aviation's last plum. In December, 1986, they flew nonstop around the world without refueling. They were in the air for 9 days, 3 minutes, and 44 seconds, and traveled 25,012 miles.

It had taken six years to create their radical nonmetal plane called *Voyager*. It was made of a lightweight composite graphite called magnamite and "a lot of high-tech glue." It weighed less than a ton, that is, less than a small automobile. It was designed by Dick Rutan's brother, Burt, a genius in pioneering aircraft design.

The only metal in the plane were eight nuts and bolts for the flexible wings and propellers. Twin booms flanked the fuselage, which supported the cabin and the front and rear engines. The booms were connected and crossed by the short forward wing and the long main wing, which was 8 feet longer than a 727 jetliner's. *Voyager*'s length—nose to tail—was only 33 feet. The cockpit was 7 feet long and 3½ feet wide. The fliers called it "a torture chamber, a horizontal telephone booth."

The plane was actually an interconnection of flying fuel tanks. At takeoff, across nearly 3 miles of runway in Mojave, California, it carried 1,240 gallons (3.6 tons) of gasoline and oil in the wings, stabilizers, booms, and fuselage.

Mr. Rutan was a retired air force lieutenant colonel, a combat pilot with 325 missions in Vietnam. "The *Voyager* was the only airplane I've ever been afraid of," he confessed. Ms. Yeager was trained as a mechanical drafting engineer, and she had piloting experience.

George Herman "Babe" Ruth (1895–1948) is hailed as the greatest player in baseball history. He single-handedly made the game the national pastime. He set or tied dozens of batting and pitching records. His feats with a 47-ounce bat he called "Black Betsy" turned the new Yankee Stadium, in The Bronx, New York, into the "house that Ruth built."

The Babe was known as the Sultan of Swat. He belted 714 home runs, 1 on the average of every 11.8 official times at bat. In 1927, he slammed 60, beating his 1921 record of 59. The 60 were more than the total homers hit by all the players on any one club in the American League that year. In a 12-year stretch, he hit an average of 46.8 pitches out of the park each year. He held first place in career homers for 47 years, until Henry "Hank" Aaron belted his 715th in 1974 (see page 1).

Mr. Ruth's career batting average was .342 and his slugging average was a fantastic .690. He walked a record 2,056 times.

Before becoming a full-time Yankee slugger, the Babe was an outstanding pitcher for 6 years with the Boston Red Sox. He is co-holder of the record for the most shutouts (9) pitched by a left-hander in one season in the American League. He still holds the mark for most innings pitched in one World Series game: He went 14 for the Red Sox, edging the Brooklyn Dodgers 2–1, on October 9, 1916. He once hurled 29⅔ consecutive scoreless innings in World Series competition. His career pitching record was 94 wins, 46 losses, with a 2.28 earned-run average.

When someone informed the Babe during the economic depression of the early 1930s that he made more money than President Herbert Hoover, he replied, "I had a better year."

Jonas Salk (born in 1914) is a miracle maker. He was a research scientist at the University of Pittsburgh School of Medicine in 1955 when he perfected the vaccine that helped to wipe out polio, or infantile paralysis.

Epidemics had crippled and killed thousands of people every year. (President Franklin D. Roosevelt was crippled by polio.) It was believed that only vaccines made of living viruses could guarantee protection. Dr. Salk produced a killed-virus vaccine from polio virus cultivated in the kidney tissue of monkeys. The Salk family were the first people to test the vaccine.

Dr. Salk also developed a flu vaccine. He is now striving to develop a vaccine against acquired immune deficiency syndrome, AIDS.

The Salk Institute for Biological Studies, which Dr. Salk founded in La Jolla, California, brings together science, philosophy, and art to help human beings learn more about human beings. "Not only is all life interrelated," he has said, "but everything in the cosmos is related to everything else. The time has now arrived when we must realize we are all part of a single organism, and we must develop some new kinds of responses to the world around us. The new world will be a world where the fittest will be those who fit best into a pattern designed to fit the purpose of nature. Real wisdom implies making judgments in advance rather than in retrospect."

Dr. Salk has been honored with the Presidential Citation and the Gold Medal of Congress.

Dred Scott (c. 1795–1858), born a slave in Virginia, thought he had gained his freedom when he moved with his owner to the free state of Illinois and later into the free Wisconsin Territory. When he then returned to a state that permitted slavery, Mr. Scott was declared by local courts to still be a slave. He became the subject of one of the Supreme Court's most controversial decisions.

A New York abolitionist by the name of John Sanford became Mr. Scott's chief supporter. They probably never met; Mr. Sanford was interested in Mr. Scott only as a means to a greater goal: freedom for all slaves. (A slave could have been freed at any time by the mere stroke of his owner's pen.)

Dred Scott (1857) was the test case by which abolitionists sought to force national law to deal at last with slavery. But the Supreme Court, in a decision that outraged freedom-loving people everywhere, ruled that a slave did not automatically become free by going into a free state; furthermore, the Court declared, blacks were not citizens and therefore could not sue in federal courts. Chief Justice Roger B. Taney declared that blacks "had no right which the white man was bound to respect" and "the right of property in a slave is distinctly and expressly affirmed in the Constitution."

Many Americans agreed that the Taney Court's decision in *Dred Scott* was the greatest political calamity that this country, under its forms of government, could sustain. It was a key factor in bringing on the Civil War 4 years later.

Mr. Scott's owner gave him his freedom. In late 1865, eight months after the slave-free North had won the war, the 13th Amendment to the Constitution abolished slavery everywhere in the country.

William H. Seward (1801–1872), President Andrew Johnson's Secretary of State, arranged for the purchase of Alaska from Russia in 1867. The 586,400 square miles cost $7.2 million.

Because few people thought it was worth the purchase price, Alaska came to be jokingly called "Seward's Ice Box" and "Seward's Folly." Alaska has turned out to be a bonanza. It is rich in oil, fishing, lumbering, mining, and fur trapping, and it abounds in natural wonders.

Alaska became the 49th state of the United States in 1959. It is the largest state. And it is also the state with the least population. Each resident could have nearly 2 square miles. (New York City residents, for a comparison, have only .0000462th of a square mile apiece.)

Mr. Seward was also President Abraham Lincoln's Secretary of State. He suggested that the United States intentionally start a war with a European nation; it would unite all the states and head off the Civil War. Such "wild" ideas are known as trial balloons; Mr. Seward's was quickly deflated.

On the night in April, 1865, that President Lincoln was shot to death by a Southern sympathizer, Secretary Seward was stabbed in the bedroom of his home by one of the assassin's confederates. He survived the attack and served in the cabinet of President Andrew Johnson.

Upton Sinclair (1878–1968) was a writer-rebel. He fought for a multitude of causes: healthy meat, strong trade unions, abolition of child labor, birth control, Prohibition, an honest press, morality in business and industry, vegetarianism, educational reform, and civil liberties.

His many books exposed corruption in American business. To learn what the meat industry was really all about, he lived for seven unforgettable weeks among immigrant Lithuanian workers in stockyards in Chicago. He was overwhelmed by the odor. He saw dead rats swept into the meat-conveyor belt and come out wrapped as sausages for shipment to consumers. His book *The Jungle* (1906) led to Congressional investigations and the first federal pure-food legislation. "I aimed [*The Jungle*] at the public's heart and by accident I hit it in the stomach," Mr. Sinclair said.

For 10 years, beginning in 1939, the author wrote a cycle of 11 nonfiction novels about a journalist hero (Lanny Budd) involved in national and international events. His "Budd book" *Dragon's Teeth*, dealing with the rise of Adolf Hitler in Germany, was honored with a Pulitzer Prize in 1942.

Mr. Sinclair believed that true social justice can be "achieved and maintained only through the democratic process."

Mark Spitz (born in 1950) won an unprecedented seven gold medals in swimming in the Olympic Games in Munich, West Germany, in 1972. He was the first competitor to win that many in a single Olympiad. His feat has been celebrated as the greatest individual performance in the 100-year history of the modern Olympics.

Mr. Spitz won four individual golds: in the 100-meter freestyle, the 200-meter freestyle, the 100-meter butterfly, and the 200-meter butterfly. He also won three team gold medals. Four years earlier, he had won two golds in the Olympics in Mexico City.

Between 1967 and 1972, the 6-footer set 26 individual world records in the freestyle and the butterfly, and he was on the relay team that established seven world records.

At the age of 39, Mr. Spitz began training for the 1992 Olympics to be held in Barcelona, Spain. He has his sights on another gold medal in his favorite event, the 100-meter butterfly.

Over the years he has never lost his speed in the water, and he stays in good shape. Training for Barcelona, he will swim about 3,600 miles, which is like swimming from Los Angeles to New York, then back to Chicago.

Harriet Beecher Stowe (1811–1896) was a social reformer who was once greeted by President Abraham Lincoln as "the little lady who made the great war"—the Civil War.

Mrs. Stowe was the author of the best-selling antislavery novel *Uncle Tom's Cabin, or Life Among the Lowly*. It was published in 1852, nine years before the war. It was based on Mrs. Stowe's observations of slavery in Ohio and Kentucky. She made the reader see clearly the evil that was slavery. The breakup of black families particularly enraged the author.

Sales of the book exceeded an astounding 300,000 copies in the first year alone, almost all in the North; at least that many people in the South hated the book.

One of the book's most famous passages is: "Eliza made her desperate retreat across the river just in the dusk of twilight. The gray mist of the evening, rising slowly from the river, enveloped her as she disappeared up the bank, and the swollen current and floundering masses of ice presented a hopeless barrier between her and her pursuer."

The famous New England essayist and poet Ralph Waldo Emerson wrote about Mrs. Stowe: "We have seen an American woman write a novel of which a million copies were sold in all languages, and which had one merit, of speaking in the universal heart, and was read with equal interest to three audiences, namely, in the parlor, in the kitchen, and in the nursery of every house."

William Howard Taft (1857–1930) is the only person to serve as the President of the United States and as the Chief Justice of the United States. He was our 27th Chief Executive (1909–1913) and our 10th Chief Justice (1921–1930).

Between his Presidency and his work as a judge, he was a professor of constitutional law at Yale University. Because he traveled extensively, he had to grade student papers on trains, in hotels, and in private homes where he was a guest.

Mr. Taft had wanted to sit on the Supreme Court much more than he had wanted to be the President. But he twice turned down an appointment by President Theodore Roosevelt to the highest bench; he was civil governor of the Philippines after the Spanish-American War (1898) and felt he couldn't leave his uncompleted work there to go on the Court. He became President Roosevelt's Secretary of War in 1904 and helped to organize construction of the Panama Canal. He became President in 1909 and lost in a reluctant reelection bid 4 years later.

In 1921, he eagerly accepted President Warren G. Harding's nomination to be Chief Justice.

Mr. Taft weighed more than 350 pounds and was the butt of many jokes, such as: No one else could go swimming in the Atlantic Ocean when he was using it; and on streetcars he would rise and give his place to three women.

In 1910, he initiated the Presidential tradition of throwing out the first baseball on opening day of the major-league season. He was a right-hander.

Jim Thorpe (1888–1953), a Sac-Fox Indian from Oklahoma, was celebrated by the Associated Press in 1950 as the greatest all-around athlete of the 20th century.

He attended Carlisle Indian School in Pennsylvania. He was twice all-American in football. He was virtually Carlisle's entire track team. Once, Carlisle traveled to a meet at Lafayette College, in Easton, Pennsylvania. Lafayette's welcoming committee was puzzled when only two men got off the train. "Where's your track team?" they asked. "This is the team," Mr. Thorpe replied. "Only two of you?" "Only one," Mr. Thorpe answered. "This other fellow's the manager."

In 1912, Mr. Thorpe starred in the Olympic Games in Stockholm, Sweden, winning gold medals in the decathlon (10 track and field events) and the pentathlon (5 track and field events). No other athlete has ever won both. The King of Sweden called the Native American "the most wonderful athlete in the world."

The following year, Mr. Thorpe was forced to surrender the medals; Olympic officials had decreed that playing baseball in the East Carolina League had constituted professionalism. "I did not play for the money that was in it," the athlete contended, "but because I like to play baseball." (Only amateurs, or unpaid athletes, are usually allowed to compete in the Olympics.) In 1973, two decades after Mr. Thorpe had died, his amateur status for the period 1909–1912 was restored; in 1983, his Olympic medals were given to his family.

He played major-league baseball for six seasons, but it was his professional football career that continued to make headlines. His exploits for the Canton Bulldogs put the Ohio city on the map. He was the first president of the association that became the National Football League.

Clyde Tombaugh (born in 1906) is the only American to have discovered a planet.

On February 18, 1930, at Lowell Observatory in Flagstaff, Arizona, he detected on photographic plates the movement of a speck 3.5777 *billion* miles from Earth. The speck turned out to be Pluto, the smallest of the nine known planets in our solar system.

Pluto is about 1,400 miles in diameter, which is smaller than our Moon. Its surface is covered mostly with ice and frost. Most of the time, it is the farthest planet from the Sun. From time to time, including the present, Pluto's orbit takes it within the revolution of the eighth farthest planet, Neptune, which then becomes the most "far out" planet. It takes Pluto 248 years to go once around the Sun; it takes Earth only 365 days.

Mr. Tombaugh spent another 13 years examining the skies, but no more new planets showed up. He made many other discoveries, however: six star clusters, two comets, hundreds of asteroids and variable stars, several dozen clusters of galaxies, and one supercluster of galaxies.

"I generally take a few looks at Pluto almost every year—not much to see," he says, "only a very dim point of light."

Sojourner Truth (c. 1797–1883), who was a slave and the mother of slaves, and who was never formally educated, was the first black woman in the nation to speak out publicly against slavery. She turned out to be a spellbinding orator. She began her speeches, "Children, I talk to God and God talks to me!"

She was born in Ulster County, New York, and her original name was Isabella Van Wagener. When she was freed by the New York State Emancipation Act (1827), she renamed herself Sojourner Truth. ("Sojourner" is a traveler, one who visits temporarily.)

She battled slavery across the land. She was a woman of great mental, physical, and spiritual strength, and she was respected by social reformers everywhere. She once said about the Constitution, "I feel for my rights but there ain't any there." (The Constitution counted a slave as only "three-fifths of a person" in determining representation in Congress. Women and Native Americans were not counted at all. When the Constitution was composed in 1787, there were about 600,000 slaves, or about 360,000 such "whole black people," in the 13 states.)

Ms. Truth's famous "Ain't I a Woman?" speech at the 1851 Woman's Rights convention reproached men for their belief that women did not deserve equal rights.

Thousands of freed slaves moved into Washington, D.C., during the Civil War, doubling the area's population. Ms. Truth was appointed a counselor to the freedmen by President Abraham Lincoln. She fought segregation by refusing to move to the back of the streetcar, that is, to sit in the section that blacks-only were supposed to sit in.

Harriet Tubman (c. 1820–1913) escaped slavery in 1849 and found freedom in Pennsylvania. When she crossed the Mason-Dixon line separating the Southern (slave) and the Northern (free) states, she looked at her hands to see if she was the same person.

Mrs. Tubman became the most famous "conductor" on the Underground Railroad, a route so-named because runaway slaves secretly traveled north "underground" from hiding place to hiding place furnished by sympathetic whites. There was a price of almost $40,000 on her head, but it didn't keep "the Moses of her people," as she was called, from going into the South time and time again—19 times in all—to escort hundreds of other blacks to freedom. She worked with leading white abolitionists, including Ralph Waldo Emerson, William H. Seward, and the fiery John Brown.

During the Civil War, Mrs. Tubman was a nurse and a spy for the Northern army. She took part in a raid that freed more than 700 slaves in South Carolina. After the North won the war, in 1865, she helped to establish schools in North Carolina for former slaves. She settled in Auburn, New York, where she founded the Harriet Tubman Home for Aged Negroes.

Gene Tunney (1897–1978), a dropout from LaSalle Academy in New York, and the world's heavyweight boxing champion from 1926 to 1928, had a genuine love for learning. He was a guest lecturer on Shakespeare at Yale University and an honorary member of the Yale Pundits, a society of wits and scholars. The boxer was comfortable in the company of literary heavyweights.

He lost only 1 of his 83 fights; it was to Harry Greb in 1922. His most sensational bouts were with the renowned "Manassa Mauler," Jack Dempsey. He knocked the heavyweight crown off the heavily favored Dempsey's head in 10 rounds in 1926 and he held on to the title in a rematch with Dempsey a year later in the famous "long-count" bout. The champ retired from the ring to become a business executive.

A buddy in the Marines in the First World War turned the boxer on to the beauty and the insights of Shakespeare's poetry and plays. "The Fighting Marine's" favorite Shakespearean play was the comedy *Troilus and Cressida*. He mastered the tragicomedy *The Winter's Tale* by reading it 10 times.

During the Second World War, Mr. Tunney was director of physical fitness for the navy.

John Tyler (1790–1862) was the first Vice President of the United States to succeed to the Presidency on the death of the elected President. During the Civil War 20 years later, he was the only one of the five former Presidents still living to turn his back on the United States and to sit in the Congress of the Confederacy of 11 Southern states.

Vice President Tyler set the precedent of succession simply by saying that he was the new President when President William Henry "Tippecanoe" Harrison, our ninth President, died of pneumonia only a month after taking office, in 1841. The Constitution was not clear on succession.

President Tyler served out the 47 months remaining in the Harrison term. He helped to bring Texas into the Union. He reorganized the navy. He ended the war with the Seminole Indians in Florida. He reached a trade agreement with China. He became the first

President to have his veto of a bill overridden and passed into law by Congress.

He chose not to run in 1844 for a full term Presidency. He believed that the federal government exercised some power only the states should have, which was one reason for his defection to the South in 1861.

The English novelist Charles Dickens met President Tyler and wrote about him in his travel book *American Notes for General Circulation:* "The President's mansion is more like an English club-house, both within and without, than any other kind of establishment with which I can compare it . . . at a business-like table covered with papers, sat the President himself. He looked somewhat worn and anxious, and well he might; being at war with everybody—but the expression of his face was mild and pleasant, and his manner was remarkably unaffected, gentlemanly, and agreeable. I thought that in his whole carriage and demeanour, he became his station singularly well."

Johnny Vander Meer (born in 1914), a fireballing Cincinnati Reds left-hander, is the only major-league baseballer to have pitched two consecutive no-hit, no-run games.

The year was 1938 and he was 23 years old, dimpled, curly-haired blond, and modest.

First, he hurled a 3–0 no-hitter against the Boston Bees in Crosley Field in Cincinnati.

His next pitching turn came 5 days later in Brooklyn, New York. Coincidentally, it was the first night game in Ebbets Field and a carnival atmosphere surrounded the turning on of the 615 floodlights. Because the pregame celebration took up a lot of time, the pitcher had to warm up three times.

Incredibly, he went out to pitch the last of the ninth inning with a 6–0 lead *and* an unprecedented second straight no-hitter just three outs away. The tension was not to be believed. Night baseball *and* pitching history in the same game!

Mr. Vander Meer nailed the first Dodger easily. He then lost his control and walked the next three batters, loading the bases. He told himself he'd better stick with his "Powder River," his name for his best pitch, a blazing fastball. He forced the next batter to bounce out, third to home, cutting down the run and preserving the shutout. One out to go. It came when the next Dodger lofted a lazy fly ball to the Reds' center fielder.

In his next outing, Mr. Vander Meer continued his no-hit, no-run streak into the third inning.

He led the National League in strikeouts three times during his career, and he fired 30 shutouts, including the two headline makers back to back. He finished up with a losing record, however: 119 wins, 121 losses.

Earl Warren (1891–1974), the 14th Chief Justice of the United States, said he would like his 16-year tenure at the Supreme Court to be remembered as "the people's court." The Warren Court was devoted to civil liberties. It reshaped American society, further integrating the black and the white societies.

In the historic school segregation case *Brown* v. *Board of Education of Topeka* (1954), the Warren Court rejected the "separate but equal" decision of the Fuller Court of 58 years earlier. The justices now declared that separate but equal was inherently unequal; schools and other public facilities must be desegregated "with all deliberate speed."

The Warren Court also supported one-person, one-vote apportionment of seats in state legislatures, banned recitation of Bible verses in public schools, and overturned restrictive state abortion laws, calling abortion a "right of personal privacy" decision.

Chief Justice Warren headed President Lyndon B. Johnson's commission that determined that one man, acting alone, had assassinated President John F. Kennedy in Dallas, Texas, in November, 1963.

Mr. Warren was elected Governor of California three times before he became the Vice Presidential candidate on the losing Republican national ticket in 1948. He was appointed Chief Justice by President Dwight D. Eisenhower in 1953, and he retired from the Court in 1969.

Mercy Otis Warren (1728–1814) was the only woman to take part in the public debate in 1787–1788 over approval of the proposed new Constitution for the United States. Because Mrs. Warren was married to a political leader in Massachusetts, she knew personally many of the important figures of the American Revolution. She never hesitated to broadcast her opinions.

She wrote with great spirit against ratification of the Constitution. She believed that the Founding Fathers did not have authority to establish institutions and laws. She feared it would "draw blood from every pore by taxes, impositions, and illegal restrictions." She feared it would endanger liberty. She called it a "many-headed monster."

(The Constitution was approved by the necessary nine states within 9 months of its composition at the Federal Convention in Philadelphia, Pennsylvania.

Women were not present at the convention; in fact, women in those days did not participate in politics, they suffered an inferior legal position, and they could not vote in national elections or in most local elections.)

Mrs. Warren was a playwright and a historian. Her best-known book was the three-volume *History of the Rise, Progress, and Termination of the American Revolution.*

George Washington (1732–1799) was "the father of his country." He commanded the armies of the 13 former colonies of England to final victory in the American War of Independence (1781). Eight years later, he became our first President. He served two 4-year terms and has been the model for all Presidents who have followed.

General Washington, who had been born into wealth, planned to live out his life on his farm at Mount Vernon, Virginia, after the War of Independence. He owned hundreds of acres and about 700 slaves. But he was persuaded in 1787 to attend the Federal Convention in Philadelphia, Pennsylvania, to help try to make the original U.S. constitution, the Articles of Confederation, work. He was unanimously chosen to be the convention's presiding officer. Four months later, by which time Mr. Washington was "quite homesick," a wholly new constitution had been written, and was soon the supreme law of the land.

Mr. Washington was the unanimous choice to be the first President of the United States. He was sworn at Federal Hall in New York City, then the nation's temporary capital, under cloudy skies on April 30,

1789. He wore a dark brown suit of American broadcloth bought through an advertisement, white stockings, shoes with silver buckles, and a steel-hilted dress sword. During his first year as Chief Executive, he was ill and disabled for 109 days. He chose the site for the permanent national capital, which came to be named Washington, D.C.

In his famous farewell address (only published, never delivered orally), President Washington warned against permanent alliances with foreign powers, a big public debt, a large military establishment, and devices of a "small, artful, enterprising minority" to control or change government.

James D. Watson (born in 1928) earned two major degrees from the University of Chicago by the age of 19. With his English science partner, Francis C. H. Crick, he announced (in 1953) a discovery that revolutionized biology. They had discovered the chemical structure of the molecule DNA—deoxyribonucleic acid, the genetic building blocks of life.

It turns out that all life forms are created from the same basic genetic material. This fact supports the Darwinian theory of evolution. (A gene is a unit of heredity, characteristics passed along from generation to generation.) "To regard DNA in a superstitious way," Dr. Watson has explained, "is to be a great handicap not only to individuals but to nations."

Drs. Watson and Crick (and Maurice Wilkins) shared the 1962 Nobel Prize in physiology and medicine. Dr. Watson's best-selling book, *The Double Helix,* relates the story of the great DNA discovery, and reveals much about the politics of science.

Dr. Watson is today the director of the Cold Spring Harbor Laboratory on Long Island, New York. He believes that "everyone should be 'DNA literate.' You should know what genetic information is, what it does, the relationship between genes and ourselves, and you should know that the 'program' that provides the information to make you what you are comes from your own DNA."

Dr. Watson is directing a national program to record the identity and position of every link in a chemical chain 3 billion links long. He wants to find the genes that lead to disease. The "facts of life" project is on the scale of the United States's Manhattan Project, which built and exploded the world's first atomic bombs which brought the Second World War to a quick conclusion.

Noah Webster (1758–1843), the son of a Connecticut farmer, compiled and published the first dictionary in America. It took him 20 years to compose definitions for about 70,000 words for his *Dictionary of the English Language*, published in 1828. It was a great scholarly achievement, and "Webster" became the last word on words.

Mr. Webster also composed *The Blue-backed Speller*. It taught millions of children to spell, read, and appreciate grammar. He "Americanized" the British spelling of words. For example, he turned the British word *favour* into *favor* in books published in the United States.

The lexicographer, or compiler of a dictionary, did many things in his life. He fought in the American Revolution against England. He was a lawyer. He was a teacher. He served in the Massachusetts legislature. He helped to found Amherst College. He wrote a popular book on epidemics. He wrote articles on politics, economics, and agriculture. He made scientific experiments using dew.

Webster's Third New International Dictionary of the English Language (1971) claims direct lineage with Noah Webster's original dictionary. It has almost 2,700 triple-columned pages and a vocabulary of about 450,000 words ranging from A to zyzzogeton, which is a genus (subdivision of a family, itself divisible into species) of large South American leafhoppers (family Cicadellidae) "having the pronotum tuberculate and the front tibiae grooved."

Eli Whitney (1765–1825) invented a machine that turned out to be a key factor in bringing on the Civil War between the Northern and the Southern states 68 years later.

The machine was the cotton engine, or gin. It could remove seeds from 50 pounds of cotton every day. More hands than ever were needed to pick the tremendous amounts of cotton that the gins could process. "More hands" really meant more slaves.

The first gin began cleaning cotton on a plantation near Washington, Georgia, in 1793, and Southern farmers quickly cottoned to it. Presently, the soft white fibrous substance became the South's principal product—King Cotton.

Most historians agree that the Civil War would not have occurred if a cotton-cleaning machine using slave labor to keep it fed was not available. Slave labor was the way of life in the economy of the South.

Mr. Whitney, whose early handiwork included making and repairing violins, created a system of mass production. His factory near New Haven, Connecticut, manufactured heavy, large-caliber muskets. The inventor figured out how broken parts of the shoulder rifle could be replaced. In the past, the entire gun had to be discarded if a part of it was broken. Whitney figured out how the broken part could be removed and a new, *interchangeable* piece installed. Every Whitney trigger mechanism, for example, could fit every Whitney musket. He personally demonstrated the technique to President John Adams. Mass production techniques became the backbone of America's industrial enterprise.

Orville Wright (1871–1948) and **Wilbur Wright** (1867–1912), brothers who grew up in Dayton, Ohio, were the first to achieve motorized, manned heavier-than-air flight. That is, they were the first to fly an airplane.

The Wrights were expert bicycle mechanics and glider pilots. In flights of fancy, they put an engine in a flying machine and went where they wanted to go, not where the wind happened to blow them in a motorless glider. They finally got their idea off the ground on December 17, 1903, amid sandy hills in Kill Devil Hills, near Kitty Hawk, North Carolina.

Wilbur won the coin toss to be the first to fly. The brothers' "crate," which they dubbed the *Flyer,* had two wings and a four-cylinder engine. The pilot lay on the lower wing. There was no cockpit. The *Flyer* moved along a 60-foot-long rail and soared into the air—for 3½ seconds. The Wrights agreed that that was not flying.

Orville boarded the plane. He flew for 12 seconds

and 120 feet. *That* was flying. After three more flights, the brothers telegraphed their press agent brother Lorin in Dayton: "SUCCESS FOUR FLIGHTS THURSDAY MORNING ALL AGAINST TWENTY ONE MILE WIND STARTED FROM LEVEL WITH ENGINE POWER ALONE AVERAGE SPEED THROUGH AIR THIRTY ONE MILES LONGEST 57 SECONDS INFORM PRESS HOME ####CHRISTMAS." (The 57 was a transmission mistake; it was really 59 seconds.) At the end of the day, the plane was overturned and damaged by wind, disassembled, packed into barrels, and shipped home to Dayton.

The Wrights were soon flying distances up to 25 miles and circling intentionally in the air. They gave birth to aviation.

On the 45th anniversary of the Wrights' feat, the *Flyer* was put on permanent display in the Smithsonian Institution, in Washington, D.C.

About the Author

Jerome Agel has written and produced more than 40
major books, including collaborations with the astron-
omer-scientist Carl Sagan, the media analyst Marshall
McLuhan, the moviemaker Stanley Kubrick, the pro-
lific Isaac Asimov, the war-peace thinker Herman
Kahn, and the inventive R. Buckminster Fuller. His
first books for young readers were the 3-book set *Into
the Third Century,* exclusive 200-year histories of *The
Presidency, The Congress,* and *The Supreme Court,*
composed with the historian Richard B. Bernstein.
His other new books are about geography, English
grammar and usage, and the 26 amendments to the
United States Constitution.